REVOLUTIONIZE

YOUR

MARKETING

INNOVATIVE TECHNIQUES FOR MODERN BUSINESSES

BY

MUJAHID BAKHT

Hardcover: ISBN 979-8-9880391-4-3

Paperback: ISBN 979-8-9880391-3-6

EBook: ISBN 979-8-9880391-5-0

Published by
Atlas Amazon LLC

United States of America

Table of Contents

ABOUT AUTHER

MR. MUJAHID BAKHT,

LIFE HISTORY:- Mr. Bakht is a mature, experienced, extremely enthusiastic, energetic, administrator and thirty-six years have proven experienced as a businessman in international marketing and public relations. Mr. Bakht is an International Real Estate Specialist, and Professional Business and Projects Consultant. He was born in Pakistan, Educated in Pakistan and USA. Presently American Citizen belongs to business-oriented family. Thirty-Seven years Resident of New York, USA.

BUSINESS HISTORY:- Mr. Bakht is a Founder & President of Atlas Amazon, LLC., Mr. Bakht is a business developer and multilingual business specialist in the Caribbean, South East Asia, and the Middle East emerging markets Mr. Bakht has served, met, and host many heads of the States. Also, maintain a close

7

relationship with investors of high net worth in the USA.

CAREER:- Mr. Bakht has been engaged with many multinational companies in the field of international real estate investment, communication, technology, diamond, gold, mining, Pre-Feb housing, wind & solar energy, outsourcing management, and project consulting along with business partners & associates worldwide. Mr. Bakht has participated in major national and international conferences including participated in United Nations (U.N.O.) conferences.

TRAVEL:- Mr. Bakht is well-traveled and visited many countries around the world.

MANAGEMENT EXPERIENCE:- Thirty-Seven years of diversified experience in project consulting, marketing, and business management. As a Director of Marketing, Director of Public Relations, Director of

International Affairs, Executive Vice President, President, CEO, and Chairman of many national & multinational companies, where he served previously. Mr. Bakht hired and trained many professionals as business consultants in international marketing and supervised them. Mr. Bakht is the author and publisher of multiple books.

CERTIFICATE OF ACHIEVEMENT; Achievement Award was presented to Mr. Bakht by Stephen Fossler for five years of continued growth and customer satisfaction from 1996 to 2001.

HONORS MEMBER; Madison Who's Who of Professionals, having demonstrated exemplary achievement and distinguished contributions to the business community, registered at the Library of Congress in Washington D.C. USA. (2007 & 2008)

HONORS MEMBER; Premiere Who's Who

International, professional business executive having demonstrated exemplary achievement and distinguished contributions to the International business community, 2008 and 2009.

CERTIFICATES; Certificate of Authenticity from Bill Rodham Clinton, President of the United States, and Hillary Rodham Clinton First Lady, USA. (July 20, 2000);

CERTIFICATE OF AUTHENTICITY; from Terence R. McAuliffe, Chairman of Democratic National Committee, Tom Dachle, Senate Democratic Leader, Dick Gephardt, House Democratic Leader, USA. (June 16, 2001);

CERTIFICATE OF AUTHENTICITY; from Terence R. McAuliffe, Chairman of Democratic National Committee, USA. (April 16, 2002).

PERSONAL MEETINGS WITH DIGNITARIES:

Honorable. Teng-Hui-Lee, President of Taiwan. 1999.

Hon. Leonard Fernandez, President of Dominican Republic. 1999.

Prince. Ahmed Fahad Al-Turki, (Saudi Arabia). 2000.

Benazir Bhutto, Prime Minister of Pakistan, 2001.

Dr. Keith Mitchell, Prime Minister of Grenada, West Indies. 2003-2004.

Pierre Charles, Prime Minister of Dominica, West Indies, 2003.

Mr. Charles Sovran, Foreign Minister of Dominica, 2003.

Robert H. O. Corbin Leader & Deputy-Prime-Minister (PNC) Guyana 2004.

Hon. P. J. Peterson, Prime Minister of Jamaica. 2004.

Dr. Kenny D. Anthony, Prime Minister of Saint Lucia, West Indies. 2005.

Hon. Owen Arthur, Prime Minister of Barbados, West Indies. 2005.

Michael de la Bastide, "Chief Justice" and President of the Caribbean Islands. 2005.

Mahmood M. Hussain, the Private Office of His Royal Highness. Dr. Sheikh-

Sultan Bin Khalifa Bin Zayed Al Nahyan, Abu-Dhabi, U.A.E. 2005.

Sultan S. Al Mansoori, Saeed & Mohammed Alnaboodah, Dubai, UAE 2005.

Ibrahim A. Gambari, Under-Secretary-General (United Nations) 2006.

Hon. Villasarao Deshmukh, Chief Minister of Maharashtra, India, 2006.

Hon. Ashok Chovan, Minister of Industries, Maharashtra, India, 2006.

Hon. Liu Bowie, Ambassador of China, United Nations, 2006.

Senator Einstein Louison, Ministry of Agriculture, Grenada.

Hon. Mark Isaac, Minister of State, Grenada, West Indies.

Hon. Brenda Hood, Minister for Tourism, Civil

Aviation, Culture, Grenada.

Wayne Smith, Mayor, Township of Irvington, New Jersey, USA.

Orlando J. Moreno, Brigadier General & Military Advisor, (UNO) Venezuela.

As well as many more

CHAPTER 1

Introduction

Revolutionize Your Marketing Innovative Techniques for Modern Businesses" is a book that provides practical insights and strategies for modern businesses to improve their marketing efforts. The book highlights the importance of adapting to changes in the marketing landscape and understanding the characteristics and expectations of modern consumers. It covers a wide range of topics, including data-driven marketing, social media, influencer marketing, content marketing, email marketing, SEO, video marketing, marketing automation, AI, customer experience, personalization, call-to-actions, marketing planning, measuring marketing effectiveness, budgeting, and ethics. Each chapter provides actionable tips, best practices, and real-world examples to help businesses improve their marketing strategies and achieve greater success. The book is a valuable resource for marketers, business owners, entrepreneurs, and anyone interested in learning innovative techniques for modern marketing.

Marketing techniques need to be revolutionized for modern businesses because the landscape of marketing has dramatically changed in recent years. With the rise of digital technologies, consumers have become more empowered and informed, making it harder for businesses to capture their attention and retain their loyalty. Traditional marketing techniques are no longer as effective as they once were, and businesses need to adapt to the changing environment to stay relevant and competitive.

Modern consumers are increasingly using the internet and social media to research products and services, compare prices, and read reviews before making purchase decisions. This shift in consumer behavior has led to the emergence of new marketing channels, such as social media marketing and influencer marketing, which require a different approach and set of skills.

Furthermore, advancements in technology have created new opportunities for businesses to collect and analyze data, which can be used to personalize marketing messages and deliver targeted campaigns. This data-driven approach to marketing has become increasingly important in today's digital landscape, as businesses must understand their customers' preferences and behavior to deliver relevant and engaging content.

Modern businesses need to revolutionize their marketing techniques to adapt to the changing marketing landscape and meet the evolving needs of modern consumers. By embracing new technologies and strategies, businesses can improve their marketing effectiveness, drive sales, and build lasting customer relationships.

The marketing landscape is constantly changing, and businesses that fail to adapt risk being left behind. In today's digital age, consumers have access to more information than ever before, and their behavior and preferences are evolving rapidly. As a result, businesses must be proactive in adapting to changes in the marketing landscape to stay relevant, engage customers, and remain competitive.

One of the key changes in the marketing landscape is the shift towards digital channels. With the rise of the internet, social media, and mobile devices, consumers are increasingly using these channels to research products, compare prices, and make purchase decisions. This has created new opportunities for businesses to reach customers through digital marketing channels, such as social media

Advertising, search engine optimization, and email marketing.

Another change in the marketing landscape is the increasing importance of personalization. Today's consumers expect a personalized experience, with tailored content and messaging that speaks directly to their interests and needs. To achieve this level of personalization, businesses need to collect and analyze data about their customers, such as their browsing behavior, purchase history, and preferences. This data can be used to deliver targeted marketing messages and personalized offers that resonate with customers and drive sales.

In addition to these changes, businesses must also adapt to the evolving expectations of modern consumers. Today's consumers are more informed and discerning than ever before, and they expect brands to be transparent, authentic, and socially responsible. They also expect a seamless and consistent experience across all channels, from the website to the physical store. To meet these expectations, businesses must be customer-centric and focused on delivering a positive and memorable customer experience.

Adapting to changes in the marketing landscape requires a proactive and strategic approach. Businesses must constantly monitor the market and stay up-to-date with emerging trends and technologies. They must also be willing to experiment with new marketing channels and strategies, and be prepared to pivot if something isn't working. This requires a culture of innovation and a willingness to take calculated risks.

By adapting to changes in the marketing landscape, businesses can gain a competitive advantage and achieve greater success. They can reach new audiences, engage customers more effectively, and drive sales and revenue growth. They can also build lasting customer relationships and enhance their brand reputation.

However, failure to adapt to changes in the marketing landscape can have serious consequences. Businesses that cling to outdated marketing techniques risk being left behind by more innovative and agile competitors. They may struggle to reach modern consumers, who are increasingly tuning out traditional advertising and seeking out more personalized and authentic experiences.

Adapting to changes in the marketing landscape is essential for modern businesses to succeed. By embracing new technologies and strategies, and focusing on delivering a personalized and customer-centric experience, businesses can stay ahead of the curve and achieve their marketing objectives. However, this requires a proactive and strategic approach, with a willingness to experiment and take calculated risks.

CHAPTER 2

Understanding Modern Consumers

Understanding modern consumers is essential for businesses to succeed in today's marketplace. Modern consumers have access to more information than ever before, and their behavior and preferences are constantly evolving. To be successful, businesses must stay up-to-date with these changes and adapt their marketing strategies accordingly.

One of the key characteristics of modern consumers is their reliance on digital channels. Today's consumers use the internet and social media to research products, compare prices, and make purchase decisions. They expect a seamless and consistent experience across all channels, from the website to the physical store. Businesses must be prepared to meet these expectations by offering a robust digital presence and a convenient and engaging online experience.

Another important characteristic of modern consumers is their desire for personalization. Today's consumers expect a personalized experience, with tailored content and messaging that speaks directly to their interests and needs. To achieve this level of personalization, businesses need to collect and analyze data about their customers, such as their browsing behavior, purchase history, and preferences. This data can be used to deliver targeted marketing messages and personalized offers that resonate with customers and drive sales.

Modern consumers are also socially conscious and expect brands to be authentic and socially responsible. They are more likely to support brands that align with their values and take a stand on important social issues. Businesses that demonstrate a commitment to sustainability, diversity, and social responsibility can build stronger relationships with modern consumers and enhance their brand reputation.

In addition to these characteristics, modern consumers are also more informed and discerning than ever before. They have access to a wealth of information about products and services, and they are not afraid to shop around and compare prices. They expect brands to be transparent and honest about their products and services, and they are quick to call out companies that engage in deceptive or unethical practices.

To understand modern consumers, businesses must be proactive in collecting and analyzing data about their customers. They can use a variety of tools and techniques, such as customer surveys, social media listening, and website analytics, to gain insights into their customers' behavior and preferences. They can also leverage the power of artificial intelligence and machine learning to automate and streamline this process, delivering even more targeted and personalized marketing messages.

Understanding modern consumers is essential for businesses to succeed in today's marketplace. Modern consumers are digital-savvy, socially conscious, and expect a personalized and authentic experience from the brands they support. By collecting and analyzing data about their customers, and by embracing new technologies and strategies, businesses can adapt to the changing needs and preferences of modern consumers, and build lasting relationships that drive sales and growth.

Characteristics of modern consumers

Modern consumers are a diverse group of individuals who are constantly evolving and changing the way they interact with businesses. They have unique characteristics that differentiate them from previous generations, and these characteristics impact the way

24

businesses must approach marketing and customer engagement. In this article, we will explore the key characteristics of modern consumers and how businesses can adapt to meet their evolving needs.

Digital-Savvy Modern consumers are comfortable using technology and rely on digital channels to research products, compare prices, and make purchase decisions. They expect a seamless and consistent experience across all channels, from the website to the physical store. This digital-savvy behavior is fueled by the proliferation of smart phones, tablets, and other mobile devices that allow consumers to access the internet from anywhere.

Businesses must adapt to meet the needs of modern consumers by providing a robust digital presence that includes a user-friendly website, mobile app, and social media presence. They must ensure that their digital channels are optimized for search engines, easy to navigate, and offer a personalized experience that meets the needs of individual consumers. By providing a seamless and consistent experience across all channels, businesses can improve customer engagement and increase brand loyalty.

Personalization Modern consumers expect a personalized experience, with tailored content and messaging that speaks directly to their interests and needs. To achieve this level of personalization, businesses need to collect and analyze data about their customers, such as their browsing behavior, purchase history, and preferences. This data can be used to deliver targeted marketing messages and personalized offers that resonate with customers and drive sales.

Businesses must leverage data analytics and customer relationship management tools to provide personalized experiences that cater to the unique needs of individual customers. This means delivering customized product recommendations, tailored marketing messages, and personalized promotions that take into account each customer's unique preferences and behavior. By providing a personalized experience, businesses can build stronger relationships with their customers and increase the likelihood of repeat purchases.

Social Consciousness Modern consumers are socially conscious and expect brands to be authentic and socially responsible. They are more likely to support brands that align with their values and take a stand on important social issues. Businesses that demonstrate a commitment to sustainability, diversity, and social responsibility can build stronger relationships with modern consumers and enhance their brand reputation.

Businesses must identify the social causes that resonate with their customers and demonstrate a genuine commitment to these causes through their actions and communications. This can include initiatives such as reducing carbon footprint, supporting charitable causes, and promoting social justice issues. By demonstrating a commitment to social responsibility, businesses can build trust with their customers and strengthen their brand image.

Informed and Discerning Modern consumers are more informed and discerning than ever before. They have access to a wealth of information about products and services, and they are not afraid to shop around and compare prices. They expect brands to be transparent and honest about their products and services, and they are quick to call out companies that engage in deceptive or unethical practices.

Businesses must be transparent and honest in their communications with customers and must ensure that their products and services meet the highest standards of quality and value. They must also monitor social media channels and online review sites to ensure that their customers are satisfied and address any negative feedback promptly. By being transparent and responsive to customer feedback, businesses can build trust and loyalty with their customers.

Multicultural Modern consumers are a multicultural group of individuals who come from diverse backgrounds and have different preferences and needs. Businesses must recognize and respect these differences and tailor their marketing messages and products to meet the needs of different cultures and ethnic groups.

Businesses must conduct market research and understand the cultural nuances of different customer segments to deliver marketing messages that resonate with each group. This can include adapting products and services to meet the unique needs of different cultures, using culturally relevant imagery and language in marketing materials

Changes in consumer behavior and expectations

Consumer behavior and expectations have undergone significant changes over the past few years, driven by technological advancements, economic shifts, and cultural influences. These changes have major implications for businesses, which must adapt their marketing strategies to meet the evolving needs of modern consumers. In this article, we will explore some of the key changes in consumer behavior and expectations and what they mean for businesses.

Mobile-First One of the most significant changes in consumer behavior is the rise of mobile devices. Today's consumers are increasingly using their smart phones and tablets to access the internet, research products, and make purchases. According to a study by Statista, mobile devices account for over half of all internet traffic worldwide.

This shift towards mobile-first behavior has major implications for businesses. They must ensure that their websites and digital channels are optimized for mobile devices, with responsive designs that provide a seamless and intuitive user experience. Businesses must also prioritize mobile payment options and mobile apps that enable customers to make purchases and engage with the brand on-the-go.

Social Media Influence Social media has also had a significant impact on consumer behavior and expectations. Consumers today are more likely to research products and services on social media platforms, read reviews, and seek out recommendations from friends and influencers. A study by GlobalWebIndex found that over 54% of social media user's research products on social media channels.

This shift towards social media influence has major implications for businesses. They must develop a robust social media presence, with active profiles on platforms like Facbook, Twitter, and Instagram. Businesses must also invest in influencer marketing and social media advertising to reach and engage with their target audience.

Personalization Consumers today also expect a high level of personalization from businesses. They want to receive personalized recommendations, customized marketing messages, and tailored promotions that are relevant to their interests and preferences. A study by Epsilon found that over 80% of consumers are more likely to do business with a company that offers personalized experiences.

This shift towards personalization has major implications for businesses. They must leverage data and analytics to understand their customers' behavior and preferences, and use this information to deliver targeted marketing messages and promotions. Businesses must also invest in customer relationship management tools that enable them to provide a personalized experience across all channels.

Sustainability and Social Responsibility Consumers today are also more socially conscious and expect businesses to be transparent and accountable for their actions. They want to support brands that demonstrate a commitment to sustainability, diversity, and social responsibility. A study by Nielsen found that over 80% of consumers feel strongly that companies should help improve the environment.

This shift towards sustainability and social responsibility has major implications for businesses. They must adopt sustainable practices in their operations and supply chain, such as reducing waste and carbon emissions. Businesses must also demonstrate a commitment to diversity and inclusion, and support social causes that resonate with their customers.

Shift towards Online Shopping Finally, the COVID-19 pandemic has accelerated the shift towards online shopping, as consumers have been forced to avoid physical stores and embrace e-commerce. A study by Digital Commerce 360 found that online spending in the US increased by over 44% in 2020.

This shift towards online shopping has major implications for businesses. They must invest in e-commerce platforms that provide a seamless and secure shopping experience. Businesses must also optimize their digital channels for search engines and implement effective digital marketing strategies to reach and engage with online customers.

Consumer behavior and expectations have major implications for businesses. They must adapt their marketing strategies to meet the evolving needs of modern consumers, prioritizing mobile-first design, social media influence, personalization, sustainability, and online shopping. By embracing these changes and adopting innovative marketing strategies, businesses can enhance their brand reputation and build stronger relationships with their customers.

Staying up to date with consumer trends and preferences is crucial for businesses that want to remain relevant and competitive in today's rapidly changing marketplace. With consumer behavior and expectations constantly evolving, it's essential for businesses to stay on top of the latest trends and preferences to ensure that their products, services, and marketing strategies resonate with their target audience. In this article, we will explore some effective ways for businesses to stay up to date with consumer trends and preferences.

Conduct Market Research One of the most effective ways to stay up to date with consumer trends and preferences is to conduct market research. This involves gathering and analyzing data on consumer behavior, preferences, and attitudes, and using this information to inform product development, marketing strategies, and business decisions.

There are several ways that businesses can conduct market research, including surveys, focus groups, interviews, and observation. Surveys are a popular method of collecting data, as they can be distributed online or in-person and are relatively inexpensive. Focus groups and interviews can provide more in-depth insights into consumer behavior and preferences, as they allow businesses to directly engage with their target audience and ask specific questions. Observation involves observing consumer behavior in real-time, either in person or through digital analytics, to gain insights into how consumers interact with products and services.

Monitor Social Media Social media is an invaluable tool for businesses to stay up to date with consumer trends and preferences.

Consumers today are highly active on social media platforms, where they share their opinions, preferences, and experiences with brands and products.

Businesses can use social media monitoring tools to track conversations about their brand, competitors, and industry trends. This can provide valuable insights into consumer preferences and pain points, as well as opportunities for product and service improvements. Additionally, businesses can use social media to engage with their target audience directly, responding to comments and feedback and building a loyal customer base.

Attend Industry Events Attending industry events are another effective way for businesses to stay up to date with consumer trends and preferences. These events, such as trade shows, conferences, and expos, bring together industry experts, thought leaders, and influencers, providing a platform for businesses to learn about the latest trends and innovations in their field.

At industry events, businesses can attend keynote speeches, workshops, and panel discussions, where they can learn about emerging trends, consumer preferences, and new technologies. Additionally, these events provide networking opportunities, allowing businesses to connect with peers and industry experts, and build relationships that can be leveraged to stay ahead of the competition.

Use Data Analytics Data analytics is a powerful tool for businesses to stay up to date with consumer trends and preferences. By analyzing data from various sources, including website traffic, sales data, and social media engagement, businesses can gain valuable insights into consumer behavior, preferences, and pain points.

Data analytics can help businesses identify patterns and trends in consumer behavior, which can inform product development, marketing strategies, and business decisions. Additionally, data analytics can help businesses to personalize their marketing efforts, delivering targeted messaging and promotions that resonate with their target audience.

Follow Industry Publications Industry publications, such as trade magazines, blogs, and newsletters; provide a wealth of information on consumer trends and preferences. These publications are typically written by experts and thought leaders in the industry, who share their insights and opinions on emerging trends, technologies, and consumer preferences.

By following industry publications, businesses can stay up to date with the latest news and developments in their field, and gain valuable insights into consumer behavior and preferences. Additionally, these publications often include case studies and best practices, which businesses can use to inform their own marketing strategies and business decisions.

Engage with Customers (Continued)

Engaging with customers directly can provide businesses with valuable insights into consumer behavior and preferences. This can be achieved through various means, including customer feedback surveys, customer service interactions, and user-generated content.

Customer feedback surveys can provide businesses with valuable insights into customer preferences and pain points, allowing them to make informed decisions about product development and marketing strategies. Customer service interactions can also provide valuable feedback, as customers often share their opinions and experiences with a brand directly.

User-generated content, such as customer reviews and social media posts, can also provide businesses with valuable insights into consumer behavior and preferences. By monitoring user-generated content, businesses can gain insights into how customers interact with their products and services, as well as how they perceive their brand.

Staying up to date with consumer trends and preferences is crucial for businesses that want to remain competitive in today's rapidly changing marketplace. By conducting market research, monitoring social media, attending industry events, using data analytics, following industry publications, and engaging with customers directly, businesses can stay ahead of the competition and deliver products, services, and marketing strategies that resonate with their target audience.

Chapter 3

The Role of Data in Marketing

In today's data-driven world, data plays a critical role in marketing. It enables businesses to make informed decisions, create more targeted campaigns, and measure the effectiveness of their marketing efforts. In this book, we will explore the role of data in marketing and how it can help businesses achieve their marketing goals.

Understanding Your Customers

Data can help businesses understand their customers better by providing insights into their preferences, behaviors, and needs. By collecting and analyzing data on customer demographics, purchasing patterns, and online behaviors, businesses can create targeted marketing campaigns that resonate with their audience. For example, if a business collects data on the age, gender, and location of their customers, they can use this information to create marketing campaigns that target specific demographics.

Personalization

Data can also help businesses personalize their marketing efforts, which is crucial in today's competitive marketplace. Personalization involves tailoring marketing messages and experiences to individual customers based on their preferences and behaviors. By collecting and analyzing data on customer behaviors and preferences, businesses can create personalized marketing campaigns that are more likely to resonate with their audience. Personalized marketing can increase customer engagement, loyalty, and ultimately, sales.

Targeted Advertising

Data can also help businesses create more targeted advertising campaigns. By collecting data on customer behaviors, preferences, and demographics, businesses can create highly targeted advertising campaigns that are more likely to reach their target audience. For example, if a business collects data on the browsing and purchasing behavior of their customers, they can use this information to create targeted advertising campaigns that reach customers who are most likely to be interested in their products or services.

Measuring Marketing Effectiveness

Data can also help businesses measure the effectiveness of their marketing efforts. By collecting data on customer behavior and engagement, businesses can track how customers interact with their marketing campaigns and determine which campaigns are most effective. This allows businesses to optimize their marketing strategies and allocate resources more effectively.

Predictive Analytics

Data can also be used for predictive analytics, which involves using historical data to make predictions about future trends and behaviors. Predictive analytics can help businesses anticipate customer needs and behaviors, allowing them to create marketing campaigns that are more likely to resonate with their audience. For example, if a business collects data on the purchasing behavior of their customers, they can use this information to predict which products or services will be most popular in the future.

Market Segmentation

Data can also help businesses with market segmentation, which involves dividing a market into smaller groups of customers with similar needs and preferences. By analyzing data on customer demographics, behavior, and preferences, businesses can identify different segments of their target audience and create targeted marketing campaigns for each segment. This allows businesses to tailor their marketing efforts to specific groups of customers, increasing the effectiveness of their campaigns.

A/B Testing

Data can also be used for A/B testing, which involves testing different versions of marketing campaigns to determine which version is most effective. By collecting data on customer behavior and engagement with different versions of a marketing campaign, businesses can determine which version is most effective and optimize their marketing efforts accordingly. This allows businesses to create more effective marketing campaigns and allocate resources more effectively.

Competitive Analysis

Data can also be used for competitive analysis, which involves collecting and analyzing data on competitors' marketing strategies, products, and services. By analyzing data on competitors' marketing efforts, businesses can identify areas where they can improve their own marketing strategies and stay ahead of the competition.

Marketing Automation

Data can also be used for marketing automation, which involves using software to automate repetitive marketing tasks. By collecting and analyzing data on customer behavior and engagement, businesses can use marketing automation software to deliver personalized marketing messages to customers at the right time and through the right channels. This allows businesses to optimize their marketing efforts and improve customer engagement and loyalty.

Real-time Marketing

Finally, data can be used for real-time marketing, which involves using data to deliver personalized marketing messages to customers in real-time. By collecting and analyzing data on customer behavior and preferences, businesses can use real-time marketing to deliver personalized marketing messages to customers based on their current needs and preferences. This allows businesses to engage with customers more effectively and increase customer loyalty and engagement.

Data plays a critical role in marketing. It enables businesses to understand their customers better, create more targeted campaigns, measure the effectiveness of their marketing efforts, and anticipate future trends and behaviors. By using data effectively, businesses can stay ahead of the competition and deliver marketing campaigns that resonate with their audience. With the increasing amount of data available today, businesses that can effectively collect, analyze, and utilize data in their marketing efforts will have a significant competitive advantage.

How data can be used to improve marketing strategies

Data has become an essential component of marketing strategies, providing businesses with valuable insights into consumer behavior, preferences, and trends. By leveraging data effectively, businesses can improve their marketing strategies, increase customer engagement and loyalty, and ultimately drive sales and revenue. Here are some ways in which data can be used to improve marketing strategies:

Understanding Customer Behavior

Data can help businesses understand customer behavior, such as what products or services they are interested in, what channels they prefer to use, and what factors influence their purchasing decisions. By analyzing this data, businesses can tailor their marketing efforts to better meet the needs and preferences of their target audience.

For example, a business might use data on customer behavior to identify which products are most popular among their customers and create marketing campaigns focused on those products. Or they might use data on customer preferences to determine which channels are most effective for reaching their target audience and allocate resources accordingly.

Creating Targeted Marketing Campaigns

Data can also be used to create targeted marketing campaigns, allowing businesses to reach specific groups of customers with relevant and personalized messages. By analyzing data on customer demographics, behavior, and preferences, businesses can identify different segments of their target audience and create campaigns tailored to each segment.

For example, a business might use data on customer demographics to create targeted campaigns for different age groups or income levels. Or they might use data on customer behavior to create campaigns for customers who have previously purchased certain products or interacted with their brand in a specific way.

Measuring Campaign Effectiveness

Data can also be used to measure the effectiveness of marketing campaigns, allowing businesses to optimize their strategies and improve ROI. By collecting data on key metrics such as click-through rates, conversion rates, and customer engagement, businesses can determine which campaigns are most effective and make data-driven decisions about how to allocate resources.

For example, a business might use data to determine which channels or messages are most effective at driving conversions, and adjust their campaigns accordingly. Or they might use data to measure the ROI of different campaigns and allocate resources to the most effective channels.

Anticipating Future Trends

Data can also be used to anticipate future trends and behaviors, allowing businesses to stay ahead of the competition and adapt their strategies accordingly. By analyzing data on consumer behavior and preferences, businesses can identify emerging trends and predict how they will impact their target audience.

For example, a business might use data to identify emerging trends in a particular industry or demographic, and adjust their marketing strategies to capitalize on those trends. Or they might use data to anticipate shifts in consumer behavior, such as increased demand for sustainable products, and adjust their product offerings and marketing messages accordingly.

Improving Customer Experience

Finally, data can be used to improve the customer experience, which is increasingly becoming a key differentiator in today's competitive marketplace. By collecting data on customer behavior and preferences, businesses can personalize their marketing messages and improve the overall customer experience.

For example, a business might use data to deliver personalized marketing messages to customers based on their browsing history or previous purchases. Or they might use data to improve their website or mobile app design, making it easier for customers to find what they are looking for and complete their purchases.

Data is a valuable resource for businesses looking to improve their marketing strategies. By leveraging data effectively, businesses can better understand their customers, create targeted campaigns, measure the effectiveness of their efforts, anticipate future trends, and improve the overall customer experience. As data continues to play an increasingly important role in marketing, businesses that can effectively collect, analyze, and utilize data will have a significant competitive advantage.

Personalizing Marketing Efforts

One of the biggest advantages of using data in marketing is the ability to personalize marketing efforts. By collecting data on individual customers, businesses can tailor their marketing messages to their specific interests, preferences, and behavior. Personalized marketing has been shown to significantly increase customer engagement and loyalty, as customers feel that the business understands their needs and values their business.

For example, a business might use data on a customer's previous purchases to recommend related products or services. Or they might use data on a customer's browsing history to deliver targeted ads for products they have shown interest in. By personalizing marketing efforts, businesses can create a more relevant and engaging experience for their customers.

Improving Product Development

Data can also be used to improve product development by providing insights into customer needs and preferences. By collecting data on customer feedback, complaints, and usage patterns, businesses can identify areas where their products can be improved and better meet the needs of their target audience.

For example, a business might use data on customer feedback to identify common complaints or suggestions for improvement, and use that feedback to make changes to their products or services. Or they might use data on usage patterns to identify features that are underutilized or not meeting customer needs, and make changes to improve those features.

Identifying New Opportunities

Data can also be used to identify new opportunities for growth and expansion. By analyzing data on industry trends, customer behavior, and emerging technologies, businesses can identify areas where there is potential for growth and innovation.

For example, a business might use data to identify emerging trends in a particular industry, and develop new products or services to capitalize on those trends. Or they might use data to identify new technologies or channels that their target audience is using, and adjust their marketing strategies accordingly.

Enhancing Customer Retention

Finally, data can be used to enhance customer retention by providing insights into customer behavior and preferences. By analyzing data on customer purchases, interactions, and feedback, businesses can identify areas where they can improve the customer experience and increase customer loyalty.

For example, a business might use data on customer interactions to identify areas where customer service can be improved, and make changes to address those issues. Or they might use data on customer purchases to identify customers who are at risk of churning, and create targeted retention campaigns to keep those customers engaged.

Data plays a critical role in modern marketing strategies, providing businesses with valuable insights into customer behavior, preferences, and trends. By using data effectively, businesses can improve their marketing efforts, increase customer engagement and loyalty, and ultimately drive sales and revenue. As data continues to become more ubiquitous and accessible, businesses that can effectively collect, analyze, and utilize data will have a

significant competitive advantage in the
marketplace.

Optimizing Marketing Channels

Data can also be used to optimize marketing
channels by identifying the most effective
channels for reaching and engaging with the
target audience. By analyzing data on customer
behavior and engagement across different
channels, businesses can identify which
channels are most effective for driving
conversions and adjust their marketing strategies
accordingly.

For example, a business might use data on
website traffic and conversion rates to identify
which channels are driving the most sales, and
allocate more resources to those channels. Or
they might use data on customer engagement
with email campaigns to identify which types of
content and messaging are most effective, and
adjust their email marketing strategies
accordingly.

Monitoring and Measuring Performance

Data is also critical for monitoring and measuring the performance of marketing campaigns. By collecting data on key metrics such as website traffic, conversion rates, and customer engagement, businesses can track the effectiveness of their marketing efforts and make data-driven decisions to optimize performance.

For example, a business might use data on conversion rates to identify areas where their website or landing pages can be optimized for better performance. Or they might use data on customer engagement to identify areas where their marketing messaging or content can be improved to better resonate with their target audience.

Improving ROI

Finally, data can be used to improve the return on investment (ROI) of marketing campaigns by identifying areas where resources can be allocated more effectively. By analyzing data on marketing spend and performance, businesses can identify which campaigns and channels are delivering the highest ROI and adjust their budgets accordingly.

For example, a business might use data on the cost per acquisition (CPA) of different marketing campaigns to identify which campaigns are delivering the highest ROI and allocate more resources to those campaigns. Or they might use data on customer lifetime value (CLV) to identify which customer segments are most valuable to the business, and adjust their marketing strategies to better target those segments.

Data is a critical component of modern marketing strategies, providing businesses with valuable insights into customer behavior, preferences, and performance. By using data effectively, businesses can optimize their marketing efforts, increase customer engagement and loyalty, and ultimately drive sales and revenue. As the importance of data in marketing continues to grow, businesses that can effectively collect, analyze, and utilize data will have a significant competitive advantage in the marketplace.

Different types of data and their applications

Data is an essential component of modern marketing strategies, providing businesses with valuable insights into customer behavior, preferences, and performance. There are several types of data that businesses can collect and analyze to improve their marketing efforts, including demographic data, behavioral data, psychographic data, and transactional data. In this book, we will explore each of these types of data in detail and their applications in marketing.

Demographic Data

Demographic data refers to information about a customer's basic characteristics, such as age, gender, income, education, and occupation. This type of data can provide insights into the general characteristics of a customer base and help businesses to segment their audience based on shared characteristics. Some common applications of demographic data in marketing include:

Targeted Advertising: Businesses can use demographic data to target their advertising to specific demographic groups, such as age or gender. For example, a clothing retailer might target their ads for women's clothing to females between the ages of 18 and 34.

Product Development: Demographic data can also be used to inform product development decisions, such as developing products targeted towards a specific age group or income bracket.

Customer Profiling: Demographic data can help businesses to create customer profiles, which can inform marketing strategies and help to personalize marketing messages.

Behavioral Data

Behavioral data refers to information about a customer's behavior, such as their browsing and purchase history. This type of data can provide insights into a customer's interests, preferences, and purchasing habits. Some common applications of behavioral data in marketing include:

Personalization: Behavioral data can be used to personalize marketing messages based on a customer's past behavior. For example, a retailer might send a customer an email with product recommendations based on their past purchase history.

Retargeting: Behavioral data can also be used for retargeting, which involves showing ads to customers who have visited a website but did not make a purchase. By retargeting these customers with ads, businesses can encourage them to return and make a purchase.

Customer Segmentation: Behavioral data can be used to segment customers based on their behavior, such as customers who frequently make purchases versus those who do not. This can inform marketing strategies and help businesses to prioritize their marketing efforts.

Psychographic Data

Psychographic data refers to information about a customer's personality traits, values, attitudes, and lifestyle. This type of data can provide insights into a customer's motivations, preferences, and behavior. Some common applications of psychographic data in marketing include:

Branding: Psychographic data can inform branding decisions, such as developing a brand identity that resonates with a particular target audience based on their values and attitudes.

Content Marketing: Psychographic data can be used to inform content marketing strategies, such as developing content that aligns with a particular target audience's interests and values.

Customer Segmentation: Psychographic data can also be used to segment customers based on shared values and attitudes, which can inform marketing strategies and help businesses to personalize their messaging.

Transactional Data

Transactional data refers to information about a customer's purchase history, such as what products they have purchased and when. This type of data can provide insights into a customer's purchasing habits and preferences. Some common applications of transactional data in marketing include:

Upselling and Cross-Selling: Transactional data can be used to identify opportunities for upselling and cross-selling to customers based on their past purchases.

Loyalty Programs: Transactional data can also be used to inform loyalty programs, such as offering rewards based on a customer's purchase history.

Product Development: Transactional data can inform product development decisions, such as developing new products based on customer demand or discontinuing products that are not selling well.

Can collect and analyze to improve their marketing strategies. Demographic data provides insights into the general characteristics of a customer base, while behavioral data provides insights into a customer's interests, preferences, and purchasing habits. Psychographic data provides insights into a customer's personality traits, values, attitudes, and lifestyle, and transactional data provides insights into a customer's purchase history.

However, it is important to note that collecting and analyzing data comes with its own set of challenges. One of the biggest challenges is ensuring that the data collected is accurate and reliable. Businesses must also be aware of data privacy regulations and ensure that they are collecting and using data ethically.

Another challenge is the sheer volume of data that businesses can collect. With so much data available, it can be difficult to know where to start and what data to focus on. To overcome this challenge, businesses can use data analytics tools to help them make sense of the data and identify insights that can inform marketing strategies.

One popular data analytics tool is customer relationship management (CRM) software, which can help businesses manage and analyze customer data. CRM software allows businesses to track customer interactions and collect data on their behavior and preferences, making it easier to personalize marketing messages and improve customer engagement.

Another popular data analytics tool is marketing automation software, which can help businesses automate repetitive marketing tasks and streamline their marketing efforts. Marketing automation software can also provide insights into customer behavior and preferences, allowing businesses to personalize their messaging and improve customer engagement.

data plays a crucial role in modern marketing strategies. By collecting and analyzing data, businesses can gain valuable insights into customer behavior and preferences, which can inform marketing strategies and improve customer engagement. However, businesses must be aware of the challenges of collecting and using data and ensure that they are collecting and using data ethically and responsibly. With the right tools and strategies in place, businesses can stay ahead of the competition and deliver exceptional customer experiences.

Tools and techniques for collecting and analyzing data

Collecting and analyzing data is essential for modern businesses to stay competitive in the market. However, with so much data available, it can be challenging for businesses to know where to start and what tools and techniques to use. In this book, we will discuss some of the most popular tools and techniques for collecting and analyzing data.

Surveys: Surveys are a popular method of collecting data from customers. They can be conducted online or in person, and can be designed to collect a variety of data, including demographic data, behavioral data, and psychographic data. Surveys are a cost-effective way to collect data and can provide valuable insights into customer behavior and preferences.

Focus groups: Focus groups are small groups of people who are brought together to discuss a specific topic or product. Focus groups can provide valuable insights into customer preferences and opinions, and can help businesses identify potential areas for improvement.

Social media analytics: Social media platforms provide a wealth of data that businesses can use to improve their marketing strategies. Social media analytics tools can provide insights into customer behavior, sentiment analysis, and engagement metrics.

Website analytics: Website analytics tools can provide insights into customer behavior on a business's website. This includes data on how customers navigate the site, which pages they visit, and how long they spend on each page. Website analytics can help businesses identify areas for improvement and optimize their website for better customer engagement.

Customer relationship management (CRM) software: CRM software is a powerful tool for collecting and analyzing customer data. CRM software allows businesses to track customer interactions and collect data on their behavior and preferences. This data can then be used to personalize marketing messages and improve customer engagement.

Marketing automation software: Marketing automation software can help businesses automate repetitive marketing tasks and streamline their marketing efforts. Marketing automation software can also provide insights into customer behavior and preferences, allowing businesses to personalize their messaging and improve customer engagement.

A/B testing: A/B testing involves testing two different versions of a marketing campaign or website to see which version performs better.

A/B testing can help businesses identify the most effective marketing strategies and optimize their campaigns for better results.

Heat mapping: Heat mapping involves tracking where customers click on a website and which areas they spend the most time on. This data can help businesses optimize their website for better customer engagement.

there are many tools and techniques available for collecting and analyzing data. By using the right tools and techniques, businesses can gain valuable insights into customer behavior and preferences, which can inform marketing strategies and improve customer engagement. It's important for businesses to be aware of the challenges of collecting and using data and ensure that they are collecting and using data ethically and responsibly. With the right tools and strategies in place, businesses can stay ahead of the competition and deliver exceptional customer experiences.

CHAPTER 4

Creating a Strong Brand Identity

In today's crowded marketplace, building a strong brand identity is crucial for businesses to stand out and attract customers. A strong brand identity helps to establish a business's reputation, differentiate it from competitors, and create a loyal customer base. In this book, we'll discuss some key strategies for creating a strong brand identity.

Define your brand's purpose and values: The first step in creating a strong brand identity is to define your brand's purpose and values. What does your business stand for? What are its core values? What is its mission? Defining these elements will help you create a brand identity that resonates with your target audience.

Develop a unique visual identity: A strong visual identity is essential for creating a memorable brand. This includes creating a unique logo, choosing a distinctive color scheme, and developing a consistent visual style across all marketing materials. Your visual identity should reflect your brand's purpose and values and be consistent with your target audience's preferences.

Create a brand voice: A brand voice is the tone and style of language that your brand uses to communicate with customers. This can include everything from the language used in marketing materials to the tone of customer service interactions. Creating a distinctive brand voice can help your business stand out and create a more personal connection with customers.

Be consistent: Consistency is key when it comes to creating a strong brand identity. This means maintaining a consistent visual identity and brand voice across all marketing channels and customer interactions. Consistency helps to reinforce your brand identity and make it more memorable for customers.

Build a strong online presence: In today's digital age, a strong online presence is essential for building a strong brand identity. This includes having a well-designed website, a strong social media presence, and an active presence on relevant online platforms. A strong online presence helps to increase brand awareness and attract new customers.

Focus on customer experience: A strong brand identity is not just about visuals and messaging; it's also about creating a positive customer experience. This means delivering exceptional customer service, providing high-quality products and services, and going above and beyond to meet customer needs. A positive customer experience helps to build brand loyalty and create a strong reputation for your business.

Importance of strong brand identity in modern marketing

In today's increasingly competitive marketplace, having a strong brand identity is crucial to the success of any business. A brand identity is the way that a company presents itself to the world and encompasses everything from the logo and visual design to the tone and messaging used in marketing communications. In this book we will explore the importance of strong brand identity in modern marketing.

Firstly, a strong brand identity can help a business differentiate itself from competitors. With so many options available to consumers, it's essential to stand out in a crowded marketplace. A distinctive brand identity can help a business establish a unique presence that sets it apart from the competition. By developing a brand identity that is memorable and resonates with customers, a business can create a competitive advantage that is difficult for competitors to replicate.

Secondly, a strong brand identity can help to build trust with customers. In today's digital age, consumers are more savvy and discerning than ever before. They have access to vast amounts of information about products and services and are quick to research before making a purchase decision. A well-crafted brand identity can help to convey the values and personality of a business, creating an emotional connection with customers that goes beyond the functional benefits of a product or service. By consistently presenting a clear and compelling brand identity, a business can build trust with customers, leading to increased loyalty and repeat business.

Thirdly, a strong brand identity can help to attract and retain top talent. In a competitive job market, businesses need to differentiate themselves not only to customers but also to potential employees. A compelling brand identity can help to attract top talent who are aligned with the company's values and mission. In addition, a strong brand identity can help to create a sense of pride and purpose among existing employees, leading to increased retention rates and a more engaged workforce.

Fourthly, a strong brand identity can help to increase the perceived value of a product or service. Consumers are willing to pay a premium for products and services that they perceive as high quality or premium. A strong brand identity can help to create a perception of quality, leading to increased willingness to pay and higher profit margins. By investing in a strong brand identity, businesses can create a perception of value that goes beyond the functional benefits of a product or service.

Fifthly, a strong brand identity can help to create a sense of community among customers. In today's social media-driven world, customers are looking for ways to connect with like-minded individuals. A strong brand identity can help to create a sense of community among customers, leading to increased engagement and advocacy. By creating opportunities for customers to connect and engage with the brand, businesses can build a loyal following that is more likely to recommend the brand to others.

Sixthly, a strong brand identity can help to create consistency across all touchpoints. In today's omnichannel world, customers interact with businesses through a variety of touchpoints, including social media, websites, email, and physical stores. A strong brand identity can help to create consistency across all touchpoints, ensuring that customers have a seamless experience and reinforcing the values and personality of the brand. By creating a consistent brand identity, businesses can build a strong and recognizable brand that is more likely to be remembered and recommended.

Finally, a strong brand identity can help to create a foundation for future growth. As businesses grow and evolve, it's essential to have a strong brand identity that can adapt and evolve with the company. By establishing a clear and compelling brand identity from the outset, businesses can create a foundation for future growth and expansion. A strong brand identity can help to guide strategic decisions and ensure that the company stays true to its values and mission as it grows.

Elements of a strong brand identity

A strong brand identity is crucial to the success of any business. It is the way that a company presents itself to the world and encompasses everything from the logo and visual design to the tone and messaging used in marketing communications. In this book we will explore the key elements of a strong brand identity.

Brand Purpose

The first and most fundamental element of a strong brand identity is the brand purpose. The brand purpose is the reason why a business exists and the benefit it provides to its customers. It is the foundation upon which all other elements of the brand identity are built.

A strong brand purpose is authentic, meaningful, and relevant to the needs and desires of the target audience. It should be communicated clearly and consistently across all touchpoints, from advertising to customer service interactions.

For example, Nike's brand purpose is to inspire and empower athletes around the world. This purpose is reflected in everything the company does, from its product design to its marketing campaigns. By staying true to its purpose, Nike has built a loyal following of customers who share its values and beliefs.

Brand Values

The brand values are the guiding principles that inform the behavior and decision-making of a business. They are the moral compass of the brand, and they define what it stands for and how it operates.

Strong brand values are clear, consistent, and aligned with the brand purpose. They should be communicated and demonstrated by all employees, from the CEO to front-line staff.

For example, Patagonia, the outdoor clothing and gear company, has a strong set of brand values that include environmental sustainability, transparency, and social responsibility. These values are reflected in the company's product design, supply chain management, and marketing communications. By living up to its values, Patagonia has built a loyal following of customers who share its commitment to social and environmental responsibility.

Brand Personality

The brand personality is the set of human characteristics that a brand projects to its audience. It is the way that the brand expresses itself and connects with its customers on an emotional level.

Strong brand personalities are distinctive, memorable, and consistent across all touchpoints. They should reflect the brand purpose and values and resonate with the target audience.

For example, Coca-Cola's brand personality is friendly, upbeat, and optimistic. This personality is reflected in the company's advertising campaigns, packaging design, and customer interactions. By projecting a warm and positive personality, Coca-Cola has built a strong emotional connection with its customers that goes beyond the functional benefits of its products.

Brand Voice

The brand voice is the tone and style of communication that a brand uses to engage with its audience. It is the way that the brand speaks and the words it chooses to convey its message.

Strong brand voices are consistent, appropriate for the audience, and reflective of the brand personality. They should be used consistently across all touchpoints, from social media to customer service interactions.

For example, the brand voice of Airbnb, the online marketplace for short-term rentals, is friendly, welcoming, and informative. This voice is reflected in the company's website copy, email communications, and social media posts. By using a consistent and engaging voice, Airbnb has built a strong brand identity that resonates with its target audience.

Brand Visual Identity

The brand visual identity is the set of visual elements that a brand uses to represent itself to the world. It includes the logo, color palette, typography, and graphic elements.

Strong brand visual identities are distinctive, memorable, and reflective of the brand purpose and personality. They should be consistent across all touchpoints, from the website to packaging design.

Strategies for developing and maintaining a strong brand identity

Developing and maintaining a strong brand identity is critical for any business that wants to build brand loyalty, attract new customers, and differentiate itself from competitors. In this book we will discuss some strategies for developing and maintaining a strong brand identity.

Define Your Brand Purpose and Values

The first step in developing a strong brand identity is to define your brand purpose and values. Your brand purpose should be the driving force behind everything you do, and your values should guide your behavior and decision-making.

To define your brand purpose and values, ask yourself what makes your business unique and why it exists. Consider what values are important to your target audience and how you can align with those values.

Once you have defined your brand purpose and values, communicate them consistently across all touchpoints, from advertising to customer service interactions. This will help build trust and credibility with your target audience and differentiate your brand from competitors.

Develop a Consistent Brand Personality and Voice

A strong brand identity requires a consistent brand personality and voice. Your brand personality should be distinctive, memorable, and reflective of your brand purpose and values. Your brand voice should be appropriate for your target audience and consistent across all touchpoints.

To develop a consistent brand personality and voice, consider your target audience and how you want to be perceived. Define your tone and style of communication, and ensure that it is reflected in all of your marketing communications, from social media to customer service interactions.

Create a Strong Visual Identity

A strong visual identity is critical for building a strong brand identity. Your visual identity should be distinctive, memorable, and reflective of your brand purpose and personality.

To create a strong visual identity, start with your logo. Your logo should be simple, easily recognizable, and reflective of your brand purpose and personality. Consider your color palette, typography, and graphic elements, and ensure that they are consistent across all touch points, from your website to your packaging design.

Build Brand Awareness and Engagement

Building brand awareness and engagement is critical for developing and maintaining a strong brand identity. To build brand awareness, consider using a mix of advertising, public relations, social media, and content marketing.

To build brand engagement, focus on creating a positive customer experience at every touchpoint. This includes providing exceptional customer service, creating engaging content, and listening to feedback from your customers.

Monitor and Adapt to Changes in the Market

Finally, to maintain a strong brand identity, it is important to monitor and adapt to changes in the market. This includes staying up-to-date on trends and changes in your industry, monitoring your competitors, and adapting your brand identity as necessary.

To monitor changes in the market, consider conducting market research, monitoring social media conversations, and staying up-to-date on industry news. Use this information to adapt your brand identity and marketing communications as necessary.

CHAPTER 5

Leveraging Social Media for Marketing

Social media has become an integral part of our daily lives, and it has also become a powerful tool for marketing. With billions of people using social media platforms, businesses can leverage these platforms to connect with their target audience, build brand awareness, and drive sales. We will discuss the ways in which businesses can leverage social media for marketing.

Build a Strong Social Media Presence

The first step in leveraging social media for marketing is to build a strong social media presence. This involves creating profiles on relevant social media platforms and optimizing those profiles to ensure they are consistent with your brand identity.

To optimize your social media profiles, consider the following:

Use your brand logo and colors to create a consistent visual identity across all platforms. Write a compelling bio that accurately represents your brand and what you have to offer.

Post engaging content that is relevant to your target audience.

Develop a Content Strategy

Once you have built a strong social media presence, the next step is to develop a content strategy. A content strategy outlines the types of content you will create, the frequency of posts, and the platforms on which you will post that content.

To develop a content strategy, consider the following: Determine your target audience and their interests.

Choose the types of content that will resonate with your target audience, such as blog posts, info graphics, videos, or podcasts.

Plan the frequency of posts and the platforms on which you will post them.

Engage with Your Audience

Social media is a two-way conversation, and it is important to engage with your audience to build relationships and foster brand loyalty. This can be done by responding to comments and messages, asking questions, and soliciting feedback from your audience.

To engage with your audience, consider the following:

Respond to comments and messages promptly.

Ask questions to encourage engagement.

Solicit feedback from your audience and use it to improve your products or services.

Leverage Influencers

Influencer marketing has become a popular way for businesses to leverage social media for marketing. Influencers are individuals with a large following on social media who can promote your brand to their followers.

To leverage influencers, consider the following:

Identify influencers who are relevant to your brand and target audience.

Develop a relationship with those influencers by engaging with them on social media.

Offer incentives such as free products or services in exchange for promoting your brand.

Use Paid Advertising

Social media platforms also offer a range of paid advertising options that businesses can use to reach their target audience. Paid advertising can be highly targeted, allowing businesses to reach a specific demographic or interest group.

To use paid advertising on social media, consider the following:

Choose the platform that is most relevant to your target audience.

Define your target audience and choose targeting options such as age, location, interests, and behaviors.

Create ad content that is compelling and relevant to your target audience.

Measure and Analyze Results

Finally, it is important to measure and analyze the results of your social media marketing efforts. This allows you to determine what is working and what is not, and to make changes as necessary.

To measure and analyze your social media marketing efforts, consider the following:

Use analytics tools to track engagement, reach, and conversions.

Compare your results to your goals and adjust your strategy as necessary.

Use A/B testing to test different types of content or advertising and determine which is most effective.

Benefits of using social media for marketing

Social media has become an essential tool for businesses of all sizes, enabling them to connect with their target audience, build brand awareness, and drive sales. In this essay, we will discuss the benefits of using social media for marketing.

Increased Brand Awareness

One of the most significant benefits of using social media for marketing is increased brand awareness. With billions of people using social media platforms, businesses can reach a vast audience, including individuals who may not have otherwise been exposed to their brand.

By posting engaging content, businesses can increase their reach and encourage users to share their content with their own followers, further increasing brand awareness. Over time, this can result in a larger audience, greater brand recognition, and increased sales.

Enhanced Customer Engagement

Social media enables businesses to engage with their customers in a more meaningful way than traditional marketing channels. With social media, businesses can respond to customer inquiries, feedback, and complaints quickly and efficiently, showing that they care about their customers and are committed to providing excellent service.

By engaging with customers on social media, businesses can also build stronger relationships with their customers and foster brand loyalty. This can lead to increased repeat business and positive word-of-mouth recommendations.

Targeted Advertising

Social media platforms offer businesses the ability to target their advertising to specific demographics, interests, and behaviors. This means that businesses can reach their ideal customer with highly targeted messaging, increasing the chances of converting that customer into a sale.

By targeting advertising to specific audiences, businesses can also maximize their advertising budget and reduce wasted spend on advertising that is not relevant to their target audience.

Cost-Effective Marketing

Social media is also a cost-effective marketing channel, particularly for small businesses with limited budgets. Many social media platforms offer free profiles and pages, allowing businesses to build a social media presence without incurring significant costs.

Even when businesses choose to invest in paid social media advertising, the cost is typically lower than traditional advertising channels, such as print or television advertising. This means that businesses can reach a larger audience and drive more sales while minimizing their marketing expenses.

Improved Search Engine Rankings

Social media can also improve a business's search engine rankings. By posting engaging content and building a strong social media presence, businesses can increase their online visibility, making it easier for potential customers to find them through search engines.

Additionally, social media profiles and pages are often indexed by search engines, meaning that businesses with a strong social media presence may appear higher in search engine results pages, further increasing their online visibility.

Access to Valuable Customer Insights

Finally, social media provides businesses with access to valuable customer insights. Social media analytics tools can help businesses understand their audience's behavior, preferences, and interests, allowing them to create more targeted and effective marketing campaigns.

By analyzing social media data, businesses can also gain insights into their competitors' strategies, identify industry trends, and make data-driven decisions about their marketing efforts.

Strategies for creating effective social media campaigns

Social media has become an essential part of any modern marketing strategy, providing businesses with a powerful tool for reaching their target audience, building brand awareness, and driving sales. However, creating effective social media campaigns can be a complex and challenging task. we will discuss strategies for creating effective social media campaigns.

Define Your Goals

The first step in creating an effective social media campaign is to define your goals. What do you want to achieve through your social media efforts? Do you want to increase brand awareness, drive traffic to your website, generate leads, or increase sales?

Defining your goals will help you create a more focused and effective social media campaign by guiding your content creation, targeting, and measurement strategies.

Know Your Audience

The success of your social media campaign will largely depend on how well you know your audience. Who are they? What are their interests, pain points, and behaviors? What social media platforms do they use, and how do they consume content?

By understanding your audience, you can create content that resonates with them and target your campaigns more effectively.

Develop a Content Strategy

Content is the cornerstone of any social media campaign. To create effective social media campaigns, you need to develop a content strategy that aligns with your goals, audience, and brand identity.

Your content strategy should include the types of content you will create, the frequency of posting, and the tone and style of your content. It should also consider the different social media platforms and the types of content that perform best on each platform.

Leverage Visuals

Visual content, such as images and videos, can be highly effective on social media. Visuals are more likely to catch users' attention and increase engagement rates.

When creating visual content, consider using high-quality images, branded graphics, and videos that tell a story or demonstrate your product or service.

Engage with Your Audience

Social media is a two-way conversation, and engaging with your audience is a critical component of any social media campaign. Respond to comments, answer questions, and thank users for sharing your content.

Engaging with your audience not only fosters relationships and builds brand loyalty, but it also signals to social media algorithms that your content is valuable and deserving of higher visibility.

Invest in Paid Advertising

While organic social media strategies can be effective, paid social media advertising can amplify your reach and increase conversions. Paid social media advertising allows you to target specific demographics, interests, and behaviors, ensuring that your message reaches your ideal customer.

When investing in paid social media advertising, consider setting clear goals and objectives, testing different ad formats and targeting strategies, and monitoring and adjusting your campaigns regularly.

Measure Your Results

Finally, to create effective social media campaigns, you need to measure your results. Measuring your social media performance allows you to understand what's working and what's not, and make data-driven decisions about your content strategy, targeting, and investment.

Social media metrics to track include engagement rates, reach, clicks, conversions, and return on investment (ROI).

Tips for engaging with social media followers

Social media has become a vital platform for businesses to engage with their audience and build a strong online presence. Engaging with social media followers is an essential part of any effective social media strategy, as it fosters relationships, builds trust and loyalty, and increases brand awareness we will discuss tips for engaging with social media followers.

Respond to Comments and Messages Promptly

One of the most important ways to engage with social media followers is to respond to comments and messages promptly. This shows that you value their input and are actively listening to their feedback. Responding in a timely manner also helps to create a positive impression of your brand and demonstrates your commitment to customer service.

Be Authentic and Personable

Authenticity and person ability are key elements in engaging with social media followers. People want to interact with real people, not just brands. Use a friendly and conversational tone in your responses, and don't be afraid to inject some humor or personality into your interactions.

Use User-Generated Content

User-generated content (UGC) is an excellent way to engage with your followers and build a sense of community around your brand. Reposting UGC on your social media channels shows that you value your customers and appreciate their contributions. It also helps to create a sense of social proof, which can be a powerful motivator for other users to engage with your brand.

Run Contests and Giveaways

Contests and giveaways are a fun and effective way to engage with social media followers. They encourage users to interact with your brand, share your content, and increase your reach. When planning a contest or giveaway, make sure to set clear rules, promote it across your social media channels, and offer an attractive prize that will motivate people to participate.

Ask for Feedback and Opinions

Asking for feedback and opinions from your social media followers shows that you value their input and are committed to improving your products or services. Use polls or open-ended questions to solicit feedback, and respond to comments and suggestions in a timely and respectful manner.

Share Behind-the-Scenes Content

Sharing behind-the-scenes content is a great way to humanize your brand and show your followers the people behind your products or services. This can include photos or videos of your team, the manufacturing process, or a glimpse into your company culture. Sharing these types of content can help to build a sense of trust and familiarity with your brand.

Use Social Listening Tools

Social listening tools can help you to monitor and respond to social media conversations about your brand, even if you aren't directly mentioned. By tracking relevant hash tags or keywords, you can identify opportunities to engage with potential customers or respond to feedback and concerns.

Show Appreciation for Your Followers

Showing appreciation for your followers is a simple but effective way to engage with your audience. Use social media to thank your followers for their support, offer exclusive discounts or promotions, or send personalized messages to loyal customers. Small gestures like these can go a long way in building a strong and loyal following.

In conclusion, engaging with social media followers is essential for building a strong online presence and fostering customer relationships. By responding promptly, being authentic and personable, using user-generated content, running contests and giveaways, asking for feedback and opinions, sharing behind-the-scenes content, using social listening tools, and showing appreciation for your followers, you can create a thriving social media community that supports and advocates for your brand.

CHAPTER 6

The Power of Influencer Marketing

Influencer marketing has become one of the most effective ways for businesses to connect with their target audience and drive sales. In fact, according to a recent survey by Influencer Marketing Hub, 63% of businesses plan to increase their influencer marketing budget in 2022. But what exactly is influencer marketing, and why has it become so powerful? in this chapter we will explore the basics of influencer marketing, the reasons behind its effectiveness, and the benefits it can bring to your business.

What is Influencer Marketing?

Influencer marketing is a type of marketing that involves partnering with individuals who have a large following on social media platforms, such as Instagram, YouTube, or TikTok, to promote your brand or product. These individuals, known as influencers, are considered experts in their respective fields and have a loyal following that trusts their recommendations and opinions.

Influencer marketing can take many forms, including sponsored content, reviews, endorsements, giveaways, and collaborations. Depending on the type of campaign, influencers can be compensated with money, products, or services.

Why is Influencer Marketing So Effective?

The power of influencer marketing lies in the unique relationship that influencers have with their followers. Unlike traditional advertising, which can feel intrusive or impersonal, influencer marketing allows businesses to reach their target audience in a more authentic and engaging way.

Here are a few reasons why influencer marketing is so effective:

Builds Trust and Credibility

Influencers have spent years building a relationship with their followers, and as a result, they have earned their trust and credibility. When an influencer recommends a product or service, their followers are more likely to believe and act on that recommendation because they trust the influencer's judgment.

Reaches a Targeted Audience

Influencers have a specific niche or area of expertise, which means they attract a targeted audience that is interested in their content. By partnering with an influencer who aligns with your brand's values and target audience, you can reach a more targeted audience and increase the chances of converting them into customers.

Increases Brand Awareness

Influencers have a wide reach and can help increase your brand's visibility and awareness. When an influencer shares your brand or product with their followers, they are exposing your brand to a new audience that may not have heard of your brand before.

Provides Social Proof

Influencer marketing provides social proof, which is a powerful motivator for consumers. When an influencer promotes a product or service, they are essentially vouching for its quality and value. This social proof can help alleviate any doubts or concerns that potential customers may have about your brand or product.

Drives Sales and Conversions

Influencer marketing has been shown to drive sales and conversions for businesses. According to a study by Influencer Marketing Hub, businesses that invested in influencer marketing saw an average ROI of $6.50 for every dollar spent.

Benefits of Influencer Marketing

In addition to the reasons why influencer marketing is so effective, there are many benefits that it can bring to your business. Here are a few of the key benefits of influencer marketing:

Cost-Effective

Influencer marketing can be a cost-effective way to reach your target audience. Depending on the type of campaign, you may only need to provide influencers with products or services in exchange for their promotion.

Builds Relationships

Influencer marketing can help you build relationships with influencers and their followers. By working with influencers on a regular basis, you can establish a long-term partnership that can lead to more sales and conversions.

Increases Engagement

Influencer marketing can help increase engagement with your brand. When an influencer promotes your brand or product, their followers are more likely to engage with your content and share it with their own followers. This increased engagement can help boost your social media presence and lead to more conversions.

Provides Valuable Insights

Influencer marketing can provide valuable insights into your target audience. By analyzing the engagement and feedback from influencers and their followers, you can gain a better understanding of what resonates with your audience and how to improve your marketing strategies.

Improves SEO

Influencer marketing can also improve your search engine optimization (SEO). When influencers link to your website or mention your brand in their content, it can help increase your website's authority and visibility in search engine results.

Allows for Creative Content

Influencer marketing allows for creative and engaging content that can help differentiate your brand from competitors. By collaborating with influencers on unique campaigns and content, you can create a memorable and impactful experience for your audience.

Overall, the power of influencer marketing lies in its ability to connect businesses with their target audience in an authentic and engaging way. By partnering with influencers who align with your brand's values and target audience, you can increase brand awareness, drive sales and conversions, and gain valuable insights into your audience. With its many benefits and proven effectiveness, influencer marketing is a valuable strategy that businesses should consider incorporating into their marketing mix.

How to identify and partner with the right influencers

Influencer marketing has become an increasingly popular strategy for businesses looking to reach their target audience in an authentic and engaging way. However, identifying and partnering with the right influencers can be a daunting task, especially with so many influencers and platforms available we will discuss some tips on how to identify a and partner with the right influencers for your brand.

Identify Your Goals and Target Audience

The first step in identifying and partnering with
the right influencers is to clearly define your
goals and target audience. What are you trying
to achieve with influencer marketing? Who is
your target audience? Understanding your goals
and target audience will help you identify the
influencers that align with your brand values and
can effectively reach your target audience.

Research Potential Influencers

Once you have identified your goals and target
audience, the next step is to research potential
influencers. There are several ways to do this,
including:

Google search: Start by doing a Google search
for influencers in your niche or industry. This
can help you identify influencers who are
already talking about your brand or competitors.

Social media: Use social media platforms like Instagram, TikTok, and YouTube to find influencers who are creating content related to your brand or industry.

Influencer marketing platforms: There are several influencer marketing platforms available, such as AspireIQ, Upfluence, and Grin, that can help you find influencers who align with your brand values and target audience.

Competitor analysis: Look at your competitors' social media accounts and identify the influencers they are partnering with. This can help you identify potential influencers that align with your brand and target audience.

Evaluate Influencer Authenticity and Engagement

Once you have identified potential influencers, the next step is to evaluate their authenticity and engagement. This is important because partnering with influencers who have fake followers or low engagement can hurt your brand's reputation and ROI. Some ways to evaluate an influencer's authenticity and engagement include:

Look at their engagement rate: An influencer's engagement rate is a measure of how engaged their followers are with their content. Look for influencers with a high engagement rate (around 3-6%) as this indicates that their followers are actively engaging with their content.

Check their followers: Look at an influencer's followers and make sure they are genuine and not purchased. You can use tools like Social Blade or Hype Auditor to check for fake followers.

Review their content: Look at an influencer's content and make sure it aligns with your brand values and messaging. Authenticity is key to successful influencer marketing campaigns.

Negotiate the Partnership

Once you have identified the right influencers for your brand, the next step is to negotiate the partnership. This includes discussing the terms of the partnership, such as compensation, deliverables, and timeline. Some tips for negotiating the partnership include:

Be clear about your expectations: Clearly define what you expect from the partnership, including the deliverables, timeline, and compensation.

Provide creative freedom: Give influencers creative freedom to create content that aligns with your brand values but also showcases their unique perspective.

Build a relationship: Influencer marketing is all about building relationships. Take the time to get to know the influencer and their audience, and find ways to collaborate on future campaigns.

Measure and Analyze Results

Once the partnership is in place, it is important to measure and analyze the results of the influencer marketing campaign. This can help you determine the effectiveness of the campaign and identify areas for improvement. Some metrics to track include:

Engagement rate: Measure the engagement rate of the influencer's content and compare it to your own content.

Conversion rate: Track the conversion rate of the influencer's content and compare it to your own content.

Brand awareness: Measure the increase in brand awareness and brand sentiment after the influencer marketing campaign.

ROI: Measure the ROI of the influencer marketing campaign by comparing the cost of the campaign to the revenue generated from the campaign.

By analyzing these metrics, you can determine the effectiveness of the campaign and identify areas for improvement for future influencer marketing campaigns.

Maintain the Relationship

Finally, it is important to maintain the relationship with the influencer even after the campaign is over. This includes:

Thanking the influencer: Show appreciation to the influencer for their partnership by sending a personalized thank-you note or gift.

Share the results: Share the results of the influencer marketing campaign with the influencer to show them the impact of their content.

Collaborate on future campaigns: Look for opportunities to collaborate on future campaigns or projects with the influencer.

By maintaining the relationship with the influencer, you can build a long-term partnership that benefits both your brand and the influencer.

Best practices for executing successful influencer campaigns

Influencer marketing has become an increasingly popular way for brands to reach their target audience and promote their products or services. However, executing a successful influencer campaign requires more than just finding the right influencers. In this article, we will discuss some best practices for executing successful influencer campaigns.

Set Clear Goals and Objectives

The first step in executing a successful influencer campaign is to set clear goals and objectives. This includes defining what you want to achieve with the campaign, such as increasing brand awareness, driving sales, or promoting a new product. Setting clear goals and objectives will help you measure the success of the campaign and ensure that your campaign is aligned with your overall marketing strategy.

Choose the Right Influencers

Choosing the right influencers is crucial to the success of your influencer campaign. It is important to choose influencers who have a following that aligns with your target audience and whose values align with your brand. This can be determined by analyzing the influencer's content, engagement rate, and demographics. Additionally, it is important to choose influencers who have a genuine following and a track record of producing high-quality content.

125

Develop a Creative Brief

Once you have chosen the right influencers, it is important to develop a creative brief that outlines the goals and objectives of the campaign, the key messaging, and the deliverables. This brief should include clear guidelines for the influencer, including what type of content to create, what messaging to use, and any specific requirements for the campaign. Providing a clear creative brief can help ensure that the influencer creates content that aligns with your brand and meets the goals of the campaign.

Foster a Relationship with the Influencer

Fostering a positive relationship with the influencer is key to the success of the campaign. This includes communicating clearly and regularly with the influencer, providing feedback and guidance, and showing appreciation for their work. Building a relationship with the influencer can help ensure that they are invested in the success of the campaign and motivated to produce high-quality content.

Provide Authentic and Relevant Content

Authentic and relevant content is essential to the success of an influencer campaign. Influencers are trusted by their followers because of their authentic voice and unique perspective. Therefore, it is important to allow the influencer creative freedom to produce content that aligns with their personal style and interests, while also staying true to the goals and objectives of the campaign. Providing authentic and relevant content can help ensure that the influencer's followers engage with the content and are more likely to take action.

Measure and Analyze Results

Measuring and analyzing the results of the campaign is essential to determining its success and identifying areas for improvement. This includes tracking engagement rates, reach, and conversions, as well as monitoring brand sentiment and tracking revenue generated from the campaign. Analyzing these metrics can help determine the ROI of the campaign and identify areas for improvement for future campaigns.

Monitor and Engage with Followers

Monitoring and engaging with the influencer's followers is another important aspect of executing a successful influencer campaign. This includes monitoring comments and feedback on the influencer's content and engaging with followers by responding to comments and answering questions. This can help build a relationship with the influencer's followers and promote positive sentiment towards your brand.

Stay Compliant with FTC Guidelines

It is important to stay compliant with the Federal Trade Commission (FTC) guidelines for influencer marketing. This includes disclosing any sponsored content and ensuring that the influencer's followers are aware that they are being paid to promote your brand. Failure to comply with these guidelines can result in penalties and damage to your brand's reputation.

CHAPTER 7

Content Marketing for the Modern Business

Content marketing is a strategic marketing approach focused on creating and distributing valuable, relevant, and consistent content to attract and retain a clearly defined audience - ultimately, to drive profitable customer action.

The benefits of content marketing are numerous, and can include:

Building brand awareness: By creating valuable and relevant content that resonates with your target audience, you can establish your brand as a thought leader in your industry and increase brand awareness.

Improving customer engagement: By providing valuable content that solves problems or entertains your target audience, you can build trust and engagement with your customers, leading to stronger relationships and increased loyalty.

Generating leads and sales: By creating content that is designed to move customers through the sales funnel, you can drive conversions and increase revenue for your business.

Improving search engine rankings: By optimizing your content for relevant keywords and other SEO factors, you can improve your search engine rankings and drive more organic traffic to your website.

Establishing authority: By consistently creating valuable and informative content, you can establish yourself as an authority in your industry, which can lead to increased credibility and influence.

Fostering customer loyalty: By providing ongoing value through your content, you can keep your customers engaged and loyal to your brand over time.

Overall, content marketing is a powerful tool for businesses of all sizes and industries. By focusing on creating valuable and relevant content that resonates with your target audience, you can build brand awareness, improve customer engagement, drive conversions, and establish yourself as an authority in your industry.

In the digital age, content marketing has become an essential part of any modern business's marketing strategy. With the proliferation of social media and other digital channels, businesses have more opportunities than ever to create and distribute engaging content to reach their target audience. In this article, we will discuss some key aspects of content marketing for the modern business.

Develop a Content Strategy

The first step in any successful content marketing campaign is to develop a content strategy. This includes defining your target audience, identifying the types of content that will resonate with them, and setting goals for your content marketing efforts. A well-defined content strategy can help ensure that your content is aligned with your overall marketing goals and is targeted towards the right audience.

Create Engaging Content

Creating engaging content is the cornerstone of any successful content marketing campaign. Your content should be informative, entertaining, and valuable to your target audience. This can include blog posts, videos, info graphics, podcasts, and other types of content that align with your brand and resonate with your audience. Creating high-quality content can help establish your brand as an authority in your industry and drive engagement with your target audience.

Optimize Your Content for SEO

Search engine optimization (SEO) is an important aspect of content marketing for modern businesses. By optimizing your content for relevant keywords and other SEO factors, you can increase your visibility in search engine results pages and drive organic traffic to your website. This includes optimizing your content's title, meta description, and other on-page elements, as well as building back links and social media shares to your content.

Leverage Social Media

Social media has become a key channel for content distribution for modern businesses. By leveraging social media platforms such as Facbook, Twitter, LinkedIn, and Instagram, you can reach a large audience and drive engagement with your content. This includes creating social media posts that promote your content, engaging with your followers, and using social media advertising to reach a targeted audience.

Measure and Analyze Results

Measuring and analyzing the results of your content marketing efforts is essential to determining their effectiveness and identifying areas for improvement. This includes tracking metrics such as website traffic, engagement, and conversions, as well as monitoring social media metrics such as likes, shares, and comments. By analyzing these metrics, you can determine which types of content are resonating with your audience and adjust your content strategy accordingly.

Embrace Video Content

Video content has become an increasingly popular and effective way for modern businesses to engage with their target audience. By creating informative and entertaining videos, businesses can increase engagement and build brand awareness. Video content can include explainer videos, product demos, customer testimonials, and other types of content that align with your brand and resonate with your audience.

Use Influencer Marketing

Influencer marketing has become an increasingly popular way for modern businesses to reach their target audience and build brand awareness. By partnering with influencers in your industry or niche, you can tap into their following and reach a targeted audience with your content. This includes creating content that aligns with the influencer's personal brand and values, and providing them with the resources and support they need to create high-quality content.

Types of content marketing

Content marketing involves creating and distributing valuable, relevant, and consistent content to attract and retain a target audience. There are many different types of content marketing, each with its own strengths and benefits. Here are some of the most common types of content marketing:

Blog posts: Blogging is one of the most popular types of content marketing. It involves creating regular blog posts that provide valuable information and insights to your target audience. Blogging can help build brand awareness, establish your authority in your industry, and drive traffic to your website.

Info graphics: Infographics are visual representations of data or information that can help simplify complex topics and make them more engaging for your audience. Infographics are highly shareable and can help build brand awareness and drive traffic to your website.

Videos: Video content has become increasingly popular in recent years. Videos can be used to provide valuable information, demonstrate products or services, or entertain your target audience. Video content is highly engaging and can help build brand awareness and establish your authority in your industry.

E-books and whitepapers: E-books and whitepapers are long-form pieces of content that provide in-depth information on a specific topic. They are often used to provide valuable information to prospects in exchange for their contact information, making them a valuable lead generation tool.

Podcasts: Podcasts are audio recordings that can be downloaded and listened to on demand. They are a great way to provide valuable information to your target audience in a convenient and easily digestible format.

Social media content: Social media platforms like Facbook, Twitter, and Instagram provide a great opportunity to reach your target audience with engaging and shareable content. Social media content can include text, images, videos, and other types of content.

Case studies: Case studies are real-life examples of how your products or services have helped solve a specific problem for a customer. They are highly effective at building trust and credibility with potential customers.

Webinars: Webinars are live online events that can be used to provide valuable information to your target audience in a more interactive format. Webinars are highly effective at generating leads and establishing your authority in your industry.

Email newsletters: Email newsletters are a great way to keep your target audience informed and engaged with your brand. They can include a variety of different types of content, including blog posts, videos, and promotions.

Overall, there are many different types of content marketing that businesses can use to reach and engage their target audience. By understanding the strengths and benefits of each type of content, businesses can develop a content marketing strategy that is tailored to their specific goals and audience.

Strategies for creating and distributing content that resonates with modern consumers

Creating and distributing content that resonates with modern consumers can be a challenge, but there are several key strategies that businesses can use to ensure their content is effective. Here are some of the most important strategies for creating and distributing content that resonates with modern consumers:

Know your audience: The first step in creating effective content is to understand your target audience. Who are they? What are their needs, interests, and pain points? What kind of content do they prefer to consume? By understanding your audience, you can create content that speaks directly to their interests and needs, which will help to ensure that your content resonates with them.

Focus on quality: In today's digital landscape, there is a lot of content available, and consumers have high expectations for quality. To stand out, it's important to focus on creating high-quality content that provides real value to your audience. This could include in-depth blog posts, informative videos, or engaging social media content.

Be authentic: Modern consumers value authenticity and transparency, and they can quickly spot content that feels overly promotional or inauthentic. To create content that resonates, it's important to be authentic and transparent with your audience. This could mean sharing personal stories, being honest about your business's challenges, or admitting when you don't know something.

Tell a story: Stories are a powerful way to engage and connect with modern consumers. By telling stories that are relevant to your brand and your audience, you can create a deeper emotional connection with your audience, which can help to build trust and loyalty.

Use visuals: Visual content is highly engaging and shareable, and it can help to break up long blocks of text and make your content more appealing to modern consumers. Using visuals like photos, infographics, and videos can help to make your content more memorable and increase its share ability.

Be consistent: Consistency is key when it comes to content marketing. By creating and sharing content on a regular basis, you can establish a consistent presence and build trust with your audience. Consistency can also help to keep your brand top-of-mind for consumers, which can lead to increased engagement and conversions.

Utilize multiple channels: Modern consumers consume content in a variety of ways, from social media to email newsletters to podcasts. To reach as many consumers as possible, it's important to utilize multiple channels to distribute your content. This could mean creating different types of content for different channels, or repurposing content across multiple channels.

Use data to inform your strategy: Data can provide valuable insights into what content is resonating with your audience and what isn't. By using analytics tools to track metrics like engagement, shares, and conversions, you can gain a better understanding of what content is working and adjust your strategy accordingly.

Overall, creating and distributing content that resonates with modern consumers requires a strategic and thoughtful approach. By focusing on quality, authenticity, storytelling, visuals, consistency, and data, businesses can create

content that engages and connects with their
target audience, driving brand awareness,
engagement, and conversions.

CHAPTER 8

Using Email Marketing to Connect with Customers

Email marketing is a powerful tool for businesses looking to connect with their customers and drive engagement and sales. With email, businesses can reach a large audience quickly and easily, and they can personalize their messages to make them more relevant and engaging. In this article, we'll explore some of the key strategies for using email marketing to connect with customers.

Build a quality email list

The first step in successful email marketing is building a quality email list. This means collecting email addresses from people who are interested in your brand and have given you permission to contact them. There are several ways to build your email list, including:

Offering a sign-up form on your website

Running contests or giveaways that require email sign-up

Collecting email addresses at events or in-store

Partnering with other businesses or organizations to cross-promote email sign-ups

It's important to avoid buying email lists or using other questionable tactics to acquire email addresses. Not only is this illegal in some jurisdictions, but it can also damage your brand's reputation and lead to poor email performance.

Segment your audience

Once you have a quality email list, it's important to segment your audience based on their interests, behaviors, or demographics. This allows you to send targeted, personalized messages that are more likely to resonate with your subscribers. Common segmentation strategies include:

Segmenting by purchase history or browsing behavior

Segmenting by demographic data like age, location, or gender

Segmenting by email engagement, such as opens or clicks

By segmenting your audience, you can ensure that your messages are relevant and valuable to each individual subscriber, which can lead to higher engagement and conversions.

Use attention-grabbing subject lines

The subject line is one of the most important elements of any email campaign. It's the first thing that subscribers see, and it can make the difference between an email being opened or ignored. To create attention-grabbing subject lines, consider:

Using personalization, such as the subscriber's name or location

Highlighting a benefit or value proposition

Creating urgency or scarcity with limited-time offers or stock availability

Asking a question or teasing a curiosity gap

Using emojis to add visual interest and appeal

By experimenting with different subject lines and analyzing their performance, you can determine what resonates best with your audience and optimize your future campaigns accordingly.

Create valuable content

The content of your emails should be valuable and relevant to your subscribers. This could include:

News and updates about your brand or industry

Promotions or discounts on your products or services

Educational content, such as how-to guides or tutorials

Personalized recommendations based on purchase or browsing history

Invitations to events or webinars

It's important to balance promotional content with valuable, non-promotional content to avoid being perceived as overly salesy or spammy. By providing real value to your subscribers, you can build trust and credibility and increase the likelihood that they'll engage with your brand.

Optimize for mobile devices

More than half of all emails are opened on mobile devices, so it's crucial to optimize your emails for mobile viewing. This means using a responsive design that adjusts to different screen sizes and making sure that your images and text are legible on smaller screens. It's also important to keep your emails short and to the point, since mobile users are often on-the-go and have shorter attention spans.

Test and optimize

Finally, it's important to test and optimize your email campaigns to improve their performance over time. This could include A/B testing different elements like subject lines, content, or calls-to-action, as well as analyzing metrics like open rates, click-through rates, and conversions. By continually refining your strategy and learning from your results, you can ensure that your email marketing efforts are always improving and delivering value to your subscribers.

Personalize your emails

Personalization is a powerful way to increase the effectiveness of your email campaigns. By using data about your subscribers, such as their purchase history, browsing behavior, or demographic information, you can tailor your messages to their interests and needs. This could include using their name in the subject line or greeting, recommending products based on their purchase history, or sending personalized promotions or discounts.

Use a clear call-to-action

Every email should have a clear call-to-action (CTA) that tells the subscriber what you want them to do next. This could be to visit your website, make a purchase, sign up for a newsletter, or follow you on social media. Your CTA should be prominent and easy to find within the email, and it should use clear and compelling language to encourage action.

Automate your email campaigns

Email automation allows you to send targeted, personalized messages to your subscribers based on their behavior or interests. This could include welcome emails, abandoned cart reminders, or re-engagement campaigns for inactive subscribers. By automating your email campaigns, you can save time and resources while delivering more relevant and timely messages to your subscribers.

Monitor your email performance

Finally, it's important to monitor your email performance on an ongoing basis to track your progress and identify areas for improvement. This could include analyzing metrics like open rates, click-through rates, and conversions, as well as monitoring for deliverability issues or spam complaints. By staying on top of your email performance, you can make data-driven decisions about how to optimize your campaigns for maximum impact.

Benefits of email marketing

Email marketing has become a popular and effective way for businesses to reach out to their customers, build relationships, and drive sales. Here are some of the key benefits of email marketing:

Cost-effective

Compared to other marketing channels, email marketing is relatively inexpensive. You can reach a large number of customers with a single email, and you don't need to spend a lot of money on printing, postage, or other advertising expenses. This makes email marketing an attractive option for small businesses or those with limited marketing budgets.

Targeted

One of the biggest advantages of email marketing is that you can segment your audience and send targeted messages to specific groups of customers. For example, you can send personalized emails to customers based on their purchase history, geographic location, or other demographic information. This allows you to tailor your messages to the interests and needs of your audience, which can increase engagement and conversions.

Measurable

Unlike traditional advertising methods, email marketing is highly measurable. You can track metrics like open rates, click-through rates, and conversions to see how your campaigns are performing. This allows you to make data-driven decisions about how to optimize your campaigns for maximum impact.

Engaging

Email marketing allows you to create engaging content that resonates with your audience. You can include images, videos, GIFs, and other multimedia elements to make your emails more visually appealing and interactive. This can help increase engagement and keep your subscribers interested in your brand.

Builds relationships

Email marketing can help you build relationships with your customers over time. By sending regular updates, promotions, and other valuable content, you can keep your brand top of mind and establish a sense of trust and loyalty with your audience. This can lead to increased customer retention and repeat business.

Increases sales

Email marketing can be a powerful driver of sales for your business. By sending targeted messages to your subscribers, you can promote products, offer exclusive discounts, and incentivize purchases. According to a study by the Direct Marketing Association, email marketing has an average ROI of $42 for every $1 spent.

Enhances customer experience

Email marketing can also enhance the customer experience by providing valuable information, updates, and support. For example, you can send welcome emails to new subscribers, provide order confirmations and shipping updates, and offer customer service and support through email. This can help build trust and satisfaction with your brand.

Increases website traffic

Email marketing can also drive traffic to your website. By including links to your website in your emails, you can encourage subscribers to visit your site and explore your products or services. This can also help improve your website's SEO by increasing the number of visitors and backlinks.

Best practices for creating effective email campaigns

Email marketing can be a powerful tool for businesses to connect with their customers, promote their products or services, and drive sales. However, creating effective email campaigns can be challenging, especially in a crowded inbox where attention spans are short. Here are some best practices for creating effective email campaigns that can help your messages stand out and achieve your marketing goals:

Define your audience

Before you start creating your email campaign, it's important to define your target audience. Who are you trying to reach with your messages, and what are their interests and needs? By understanding your audience, you can create content that resonates with them and drives engagement.

157

Use a clear and compelling subject line

The subject line is the first thing that subscribers will see when they receive your email, so it's important to make it clear and compelling. Use language that is concise and attention-grabbing, and avoid using clickbait or spammy language that can turn off subscribers.

Personalize your messages

Personalization can help increase engagement and drive conversions. Use subscriber data to personalize your messages with their name, location, or other relevant information. You can also segment your audience based on their interests or behavior to send more targeted messages.

Use engaging and relevant content

The content of your email should be engaging, relevant, and valuable to your audience. Use a mix of text, images, and other multimedia elements to make your messages visually appealing and interactive. Include a clear call-to-action (CTA) that encourages subscribers to take action, such as making a purchase or visiting your website.

Optimize for mobile

More than half of all emails are opened on mobile devices, so it's important to optimize your email campaigns for mobile. Use a responsive design that adjusts to different screen sizes, and make sure your content is easy to read and interact with on a small screen.

Test and measure your campaigns

Testing and measuring your email campaigns is essential for optimizing your results. A/B test different elements of your messages, such as subject lines, CTAs, and content, to see what resonates best with your audience. Use analytics tools to measure your open rates, click-through rates, and conversions, and use this data to refine your campaigns over time.

Maintain a clean and organized email list

Maintaining a clean and organized email list is important for ensuring that your messages are delivered to your subscribers' inboxes and avoiding being marked as spam. Regularly clean your list by removing inactive or bounced email addresses, and make sure you are complying with spam laws and regulations.

Use automation and segmentation

Automation and segmentation can help streamline your email marketing efforts and make your campaigns more targeted and effective. Use automation to send triggered messages based on subscriber behavior, such as abandoned cart reminders or welcome emails. Segment your audience based on their interests or behavior to send more targeted messages that are tailored to their needs and preferences.

By following these best practices, you can create effective email campaigns that engage your audience, drive conversions, and help you achieve your marketing goals. Remember to continually test and refine your campaigns over time to optimize your results and stay ahead of the competition.

Tips for building and maintaining an engaged email list

Building and maintaining an engaged email list is essential for the success of your email marketing campaigns. A high-quality email list can help you reach your target audience, build relationships with your subscribers, and drive conversions. Here are some tips for building and maintaining an engaged email list:

Use a sign-up form on your website

One of the easiest ways to start building your email list is by using a sign-up form on your website. Make sure the form is prominent and easy to find, and include a clear value proposition that explains why someone should sign up for your emails. You can also offer incentives, such as a discount or exclusive content, to encourage sign-ups.

Leverage social media

Social media can be a powerful tool for driving email sign-ups. Use your social media channels to promote your email list and share links to your sign-up form. You can also create social media ads that target your ideal audience and encourage them to sign up for your emails.

Collect email addresses offline

Don't forget about the power of offline channels for collecting email addresses. You can collect email addresses at events, in-store, or during customer service interactions. Just make sure to get permission from people before adding them to your email list.

Create valuable content

One of the best ways to keep your email list engaged is by creating valuable content that your subscribers will look forward to receiving. This can include informative articles, helpful tips, or exclusive offers. Make sure your content is relevant to your audience and aligns with your brand.

Personalize your emails

Personalization can help increase engagement and build relationships with your subscribers. Use subscriber data to personalize your emails with their name, location, or other relevant information. You can also segment your email list based on subscriber interests or behavior to send more targeted messages.

Send emails regularly

Consistency is key when it comes to maintaining an engaged email list. Make sure to send emails regularly, whether that's weekly, bi-weekly, or monthly. You can also set up automated emails, such as welcome emails or abandoned cart reminders, to keep your subscribers engaged even when you're not sending regular campaigns.

Make it easy to unsubscribe

While you want to keep your subscribers engaged, it's also important to make it easy for them to unsubscribe if they no longer want to receive your emails. Include an unsubscribe link in every email, and make sure the process is simple and straightforward.

Monitor your email metrics

Monitoring your email metrics can help you understand how engaged your email list is and identify areas for improvement. Keep track of your open rates, click-through rates, and unsubscribe rates, and use this data to refine your email campaigns over time.

By following these tips, you can build and maintain an engaged email list that will help you achieve your marketing goals and drive success for your business. Remember to focus on providing value to your subscribers, personalizing your messages, and monitoring your metrics to optimize your results over time.

CHAPTER 9

Leveraging SEO to Boost Your Online Presence

Search engine optimization (SEO) is the process of optimizing your website and its content to improve its ranking in search engine results pages (SERPs). Leveraging SEO is essential for boosting your online presence, as it can help your website appear higher in search results and drive more traffic to your site. Here are some tips for leveraging SEO to boost your online presence:

Conduct keyword research

Keyword research is the process of identifying the keywords and phrases that your target audience is searching for. By optimizing your website and its content for these keywords, you can improve your chances of appearing in relevant search results. Use tools like Google Keyword Planner or SEMrush to identify high-traffic, low-competition keywords that are relevant to your business.

Optimize your website structure

The structure of your website can have a significant impact on its search engine rankings. Make sure your website is well-organized and easy to navigate, with a clear hierarchy of pages and sections. Use descriptive, keyword-rich titles and meta descriptions for each page, and make sure your website is mobile-friendly and fast-loading.

Create high-quality content

Creating high-quality, informative content is essential for both engaging your audience and boosting your search engine rankings. Create content that is relevant to your target audience and optimized for your target keywords. Use headings, bullet points, and other formatting techniques to make your content easy to read and scan. You can also include internal links to other relevant pages on your website to help search engines understand the structure of your site.

Build backlinks

Backlinks are links from other websites to your own website. They are a critical factor in search engine rankings, as they signal to search engines that your website is authoritative and relevant. Build backlinks by creating high-quality content that other websites will want to link to, and by reaching out to other websites in your industry and asking them to link to your content.

Monitor your analytics

Monitoring your website's analytics is essential for understanding how your SEO efforts are affecting your online presence. Use tools like Google Analytics to track your website's traffic, search engine rankings, and other key metrics.

Use this data to identify areas for improvement and refine your SEO strategy over time.

Stay up-to-date with SEO best practices

SEO is a constantly evolving field, with new best practices and algorithm updates emerging regularly. Stay up-to-date with the latest SEO news and trends, and make sure your website and content are optimized according to the latest best practices. This can include techniques like optimizing for voice search, using schema markup, and creating video content.

By leveraging SEO to boost your online presence, you can improve your website's search engine rankings, drive more traffic to your site, and reach your target audience more effectively. Remember to focus on creating high-quality content, building backlinks, and monitoring your analytics to optimize your results over time.

Importance of SEO in modern marketing

Search engine optimization (SEO) is a crucial component of modern marketing, as it helps businesses improve their visibility and reach in search engine results pages (SERPs). Here are some of the key reasons why SEO is so **important in modern marketing**

Increased visibility and traffic: SEO helps businesses improve their visibility in search results, which can drive more traffic to their website. By appearing higher in search results for relevant keywords, businesses can attract more potential customers and increase their chances of generating leads and sales.

Cost-effective marketing: SEO is a cost-effective marketing strategy, as it does not require businesses to pay for advertising or other promotional activities. Instead, businesses can optimize their website and content for search engines and generate organic traffic over time.

Better user experience: SEO is not just about optimizing for search engines - it also involves creating a better user experience for website visitors. By optimizing website speed, navigation, and content, businesses can improve the user experience and increase the likelihood that visitors will stay on their site and convert.

Improved credibility and authority: By appearing higher in search results, businesses can improve their credibility and authority in their industry. Customers are more likely to trust businesses that appear at the top of search results, and businesses can use SEO to establish themselves as thought leaders and experts in their field.

Competitive advantage: In today's digital landscape, businesses must compete for online visibility and customer attention. SEO can provide a competitive advantage by helping businesses outperform their competitors in search results and reach more potential customers.

Long-term results: While SEO may take time to generate results, it can provide long-term benefits for businesses. By consistently optimizing their website and content for search engines, businesses can generate organic traffic over time and establish a strong online presence that can help them succeed in the long run.

Overall, SEO is a critical component of modern marketing, as it can help businesses improve their visibility, drive more traffic to their website, and establish themselves as credible and authoritative thought leaders in their industry. By prioritizing SEO in their marketing strategy, businesses can gain a competitive advantage and succeed in today's digital landscape.

Tips for optimizing your website and content for search engines

Optimizing your website and content for search engines is an important part of any digital marketing strategy. Here are some tips for optimizing your website and content for search engines:

Conduct keyword research: Use tools like Google Keyword Planner, SEMrush, or Ahrefs to identify relevant keywords and phrases that your target audience is searching for. Use these keywords to optimize your website and content.

Optimize website structure: Make sure your website is structured in a way that makes it easy for search engines to crawl and understand. Use clear and descriptive URLs, header tags (H1, H2, H3), and internal linking to help search engines understand the content on your site.

Optimize meta tags: Meta tags such as the title tag and meta description can influence how your website appears in search results. Use descriptive and compelling meta tags that include your target keywords.

Create high-quality content: Search engines prioritize high-quality, relevant, and valuable content. Make sure your content is well-written, informative, and engaging. Use a variety of content formats such as blog posts, videos, infographics, and more to keep your audience engaged.

Use descriptive alt tags: Alt tags help search engines understand the content of images on your website. Use descriptive alt tags that include your target keywords.

Use schema markup: Schema markup is a type of structured data that helps search engines understands the content on your website. Use schema markup to provide additional context and information about your content.

Build high-quality backlinks: Backlinks are links from other websites that point to your website. High-quality backlinks can improve your website's authority and visibility in search results. Focus on building high-quality backlinks from reputable sources.

Optimize for mobile: With the majority of internet traffic coming from mobile devices, it's important to optimize your website for mobile users. Make sure your website is mobile-responsive, loads quickly, and provides a seamless user experience.

Monitor and analyze performance: Use tools like Google Analytics and Google Search Console to monitor and analyze your website's performance in search results. Use this data to identify areas for improvement and adjust your strategy accordingly.

By following these tips, you can optimize your website and content for search engines and improve your visibility and reach in search results. Remember that SEO is an ongoing process, so it's important to regularly monitor and adjust your strategy to ensure long-term success.

Best practices for building high-quality backlinks

Backlinks, also known as inbound links or incoming links, are an essential component of any successful SEO strategy. Backlinks are links from external websites that point to your website, indicating to search engines that your website is authoritative and trustworthy. However, not all backlinks are created equal, and building high-quality backlinks is crucial for improving your website's search engine rankings and driving traffic to your site.

Focus on relevance and authority

Relevance and authority are two critical factors in building high-quality backlinks. Backlinks from relevant and authoritative websites are more valuable than those from irrelevant or low-quality sites. A relevant site is one that is related to your niche or industry, while an authoritative site is one that has a high domain authority score.

When building backlinks, focus on finding relevant and authoritative websites in your niche or industry. The more relevant and authoritative the site, the more valuable the backlink will be.

Create high-quality content

One of the best ways to attract high-quality backlinks is to create high-quality content. High-quality content is content that is informative, engaging, and shareable. When you create high-quality content, people are more likely to link to it and share it on social media, increasing your website's visibility and credibility.

To create high-quality content, conduct research, provide in-depth analysis, and include visuals such as images, videos, and infographics. Make sure your content is well-written and easy to read, and provide value to your target audience.

Use guest blogging

Guest blogging is an effective way to build high-quality backlinks. Guest blogging involves writing and publishing articles on other websites in your niche or industry, with a link back to your website.

To use guest blogging, identify relevant and authoritative websites in your niche or industry that accept guest posts. Contact the site owner or editor and pitch your article idea. Once your article is published, make sure to promote it on social media and other channels to attract more backlinks and traffic.

Use broken link building

Broken link building is a technique that involves finding broken links on other websites and replacing them with your own content. Broken links are links that no longer work, and they can harm a website's SEO. By finding broken links and replacing them with your own content, you can provide value to the website owner and attract high-quality backlinks.

To use broken link building, use a tool like Ahrefs or SEMrush to find broken links on relevant and authoritative websites in your niche or industry. Create content that is similar to the broken link's content, and reach out to the website owner or editor and suggest your content as a replacement for the broken link.

Participate in forums and online communities

Participating in forums and online communities in your niche or industry is an excellent way to build high-quality backlinks. By providing valuable insights and answering questions, you can establish yourself as an authority in your niche or industry and attract backlinks to your website.

To participate in forums and online communities, identify relevant and authoritative websites and sign up for their forums or online communities. Participate in discussions, answer questions, and provide value to the community. Make sure to include a link back to your website in your forum signature or bio.

Use social media

Social media is an excellent way to build high-quality backlinks. By sharing your content on social media platforms such as Twitter, Facbook, and LinkedIn, you can attract backlinks and increase your website's visibility.

To use social media, create social media profiles for your business and share your content on a regular basis. Engage with your followers, respond to comments and questions, and promote your content to attract backlinks and traffic.

Monitor your backlinks

Monitoring your backlinks is crucial for ensuring that they remain high-quality and relevant. Regularly monitoring your backlinks can help you identify any low-quality or spammy backlinks and take action to remove them.

Use a tool like Ahrefs or SEMrush to monitor your backlinks and track their quality and relevance. Identify any backlinks from low-quality or spammy websites and take action to remove them. Additionally, monitor your competitors' backlinks to identify new linking opportunities and stay ahead of the competition.

Diversify your backlink sources

Diversifying your backlink sources is essential for building a strong and natural backlink profile. Avoid getting all your backlinks from a single source, as it can appear spammy to search engines. Instead, focus on getting backlinks from a variety of sources such as blogs, news sites, directories, and social media.

Focus on quality over quantity

While it's important to build a strong backlink profile, it's crucial to focus on quality over quantity. A few high-quality and relevant backlinks are more valuable than many low-quality and irrelevant backlinks. Avoid getting backlinks from irrelevant or low-quality websites, as they can harm your website's reputation and search engine rankings.

Build relationships with other websites

Building relationships with other websites in your niche or industry is an excellent way to attract high-quality backlinks. Networking with other website owners, bloggers, and influencers can help you build a strong online presence, increase your visibility, and attract backlinks.

To build relationships with other websites, engage with them on social media, comment on their blog posts, and offer to collaborate on content. By building a strong relationship with other websites, you can attract natural and high-quality backlinks to your website.

CHAPTER 10

Harnessing the Power of Video Marketing

Video marketing has become an increasingly popular and effective strategy for businesses looking to promote their brand, products, and services. Video content has been shown to be more engaging, memorable, and shareable than other forms of content, making it a powerful tool for capturing your audience's attention and driving conversions. In this article, we'll explore some best practices for harnessing the power of video marketing.

Define your goals and target audience

Before you start creating video content, it's important to define your goals and target audience. What message do you want to convey with your videos? Who is your target audience, and what are their interests and preferences? Answering these questions can help you create content that resonates with your audience and drives the desired results.

Create high-quality video content

Creating high-quality video content is essential for engaging your audience and making a lasting impression. Invest in high-quality equipment, such as cameras, lighting, and microphones, to ensure that your videos look and sound professional. Additionally, focus on creating content that is visually appealing, informative, and entertaining.

Optimize your videos for SEO

Optimizing your videos for search engines can help increase their visibility and attract more views. Use relevant keywords in your video titles, descriptions, and tags to help search engines understand the content of your videos. Additionally, include links to your website or other relevant pages in your video descriptions to drive traffic and improve your website's search engine rankings.

Promote your videos on social media

Promoting your videos on social media is a great way to reach a wider audience and increase engagement. Share your videos on your social media channels, such as Facbook, Twitter, and Instagram, and encourage your followers to like, comment, and share your content. Additionally, consider running paid social media ads to target specific audiences and drive more traffic to your website.

Monitor and analyze your video performance

Monitoring and analyzing your video performance can help you understand what's working and what's not, and make data-driven decisions to improve your video marketing strategy. Use analytics tools, such as YouTube Analytics or Google Analytics, to track your video views, engagement, and conversions. Additionally, monitor social media metrics, such as likes, comments, and shares, to gauge your content's popularity and adjust your strategy accordingly.

Benefits of video marketing

Video marketing has become increasingly popular over the past few years, and for good reason. Videos have been shown to be a highly effective way to engage audiences, increase brand awareness, and drive conversions. In this article, we'll explore some of the benefits of video marketing.

Increased engagement

Videos are more engaging than other forms of content, such as text and images. They can capture your audience's attention and hold it for longer periods of time. This increased engagement can help you build a stronger connection with your audience and increase the chances of them taking action, such as making a purchase or signing up for a newsletter.

Better storytelling

Video allows you to tell a story in a way that other forms of content cannot. You can use visual and audio cues to create an emotional connection with your audience and convey your message in a way that is memorable and impactful. This storytelling approach can help you differentiate your brand from competitors and create a strong brand identity.

Increased reach

Videos have the potential to reach a wider audience than other forms of content. With platforms like YouTube and social media, your videos can be shared and discovered by people who may not have come across your brand otherwise. Additionally, video content can be easily shared by your audience, increasing its reach even further.

Increased conversions

Videos can be highly effective at driving conversions, such as purchases or sign-ups. By showcasing your products or services in action and providing valuable information, you can increase the chances of your audience taking action. Additionally, videos can help build trust with your audience, making them more likely to convert.

Improved SEO

Videos can also have a positive impact on your website's search engine rankings. Google and other search engines prioritize websites with video content, as it is seen as a valuable form of content. Additionally, videos can increase the amount of time people spend on your website, which can improve your website's overall SEO.

Better communication

Video can be an effective way to communicate complex information in a way that is easy to understand. Whether you are explaining a product or service, providing a tutorial, or sharing information about your brand, video can help you communicate your message more effectively.

Increased brand awareness

Video can help increase your brand's visibility and awareness. By creating engaging and shareable videos, you can attract new audiences and increase the chances of them becoming customers. Additionally, video can help you differentiate your brand from competitors and establish a unique identity.

Strategies for creating engaging video content

Creating engaging video content is essential for businesses looking to make an impact with their marketing efforts. Video has become a popular medium for engaging with audiences, and for good reason. Video content can help businesses tell their story, build their brand, and drive conversions. In this article, we will explore some strategies for creating engaging video content.

Know your audience

Before creating any video content, it's essential to understand who your audience is and what they want to see. What are their pain points, interests, and values? What type of content do they engage with the most? Understanding your audience will help you create video content that resonates with them and encourages them to take action.

Tell a story

One of the most effective ways to engage your audience is through storytelling. Stories help to create an emotional connection with your audience, making them more likely to remember and share your message. When creating video content, consider how you can tell a story that is relevant to your brand and resonates with your audience.

Keep it short and sweet

Attention spans are short, so it's important to keep your video content short and to the point. Focus on conveying your message in the shortest amount of time possible while still keeping your content engaging and informative.

Use high-quality visuals

Visuals are critical in video content. Poor quality visuals can turn off your audience and undermine your brand. Use high-quality visuals that are relevant to your message and brand identity. Consider using professional videographers or investing in equipment that can help you produce high-quality content.

Incorporate music and sound

Music and sound can significantly enhance the emotional impact of your video content. Music can help set the tone and mood for your content, and sound effects can help to create a more immersive experience for your audience. When choosing music and sound effects, consider your brand identity and the tone you want to set for your video content.

Provide value

Your video content should provide value to your audience. Whether it's educational, informative, or entertaining, your content should provide something that your audience wants or needs. By providing value, you can build trust with your audience and encourage them to engage with your brand.

Use humor

Humor can be an effective way to engage your audience and make your video content more memorable. Consider incorporating humor that is appropriate for your brand and audience.

Use text and graphics

Text and graphics can help to reinforce your message and make it more engaging for your audience. Consider incorporating text and graphics that are relevant to your message and brand identity.

Include a call to action

A call to action (CTA) is a crucial element of any video content. A CTA encourages your audience to take action, such as making a purchase or signing up for a newsletter. Be clear and concise with your CTA and make it easy for your audience to take action.

Promote your video content

Finally, it's essential to promote your video content to ensure that it reaches your target audience. Share your content on social media, include it in email campaigns, and consider using paid advertising to increase its reach.

Tips for promoting and distributing video content

Creating engaging video content is only half the battle. Once you've created your video, you need to make sure it reaches your target audience. In this article, we will explore some tips for promoting and distributing your video content.

Utilize social media

Social media platforms are an excellent way to promote your video content. Share your video on your brand's social media channels, and consider paid advertising on social media platforms to increase the reach of your content. You can also consider partnering with influencers to share your video content with their followers.

Optimize for search engines

Search engine optimization (SEO) is an important factor in ensuring your video content is easily discoverable by your target audience. Use relevant keywords in your video title, description, and tags, and include a transcript of your video to make it more accessible to search engines.

Email marketing

Email marketing is an effective way to distribute your video content to your audience. Include a link to your video in your email campaigns and newsletters, and consider segmenting your email list to ensure the right audience receives your content.

Utilize video hosting platforms

Video hosting platforms like YouTube and Vimeo are excellent places to distribute and promote your video content. These platforms have large audiences and can help your content reach a wider audience. Be sure to optimize your video for these platforms by using relevant keywords, descriptions, and tags.

Repurpose your content

Repurposing your video content can help you reach a wider audience and get more value from your content. Consider breaking down longer videos into shorter clips for social media or creating blog posts based on your video content.

Collaborate with other brands

Collaborating with other brands can help you reach a wider audience and build relationships within your industry. Consider partnering with other brands to create video content that is relevant to your audiences and promotes your brands.

Use paid advertising

Paid advertising is an effective way to increase the reach of your video content. Consider using paid advertising on social media platforms, search engines, and video hosting platforms to increase the visibility of your content.

Embed on your website

Embedding your video on your website is an effective way to increase engagement and keep visitors on your site. Be sure to optimize your video for website viewing by keeping it short, including a clear CTA, and ensuring it's mobile-friendly.

CHAPTER 11

The Future of Marketing Automation

Marketing automation technology is a powerful tool that helps businesses automate repetitive marketing tasks and streamline communication with customers. The technology combines software and tactics that allow businesses to deliver personalized experiences to customers while improving efficiency and effectiveness.

Customer Relationship Management (CRM) System

A CRM system is the foundation of marketing automation. It stores customer data, tracks interactions, and helps businesses identify opportunities to engage with customers. By integrating with other marketing automation tools, businesses can create automated workflows that streamline communication with customers.

Email Marketing Automation

Email marketing automation tools allow businesses to create personalized email campaigns based on customer behavior and preferences. By segmenting customers and sending targeted messages, businesses can increase open and click-through rates and drive conversions.

Social Media Management

Social media management tools allow businesses to manage and automate social media accounts. By scheduling posts, tracking engagement, and analyzing data, businesses can improve their social media strategy and reach a larger audience.

Landing Pages and Forms

Landing pages and forms are essential for capturing customer information and generating leads. Marketing automation tools allow businesses to create landing pages and forms that are optimized for conversions and integrate with CRM systems to track lead activity.

Lead Scoring and Nurturing

Lead scoring and nurturing tools allow businesses to prioritize leads based on their level of engagement and readiness to purchase. By tracking customer behavior and interactions, businesses can deliver targeted messages that move leads through the sales funnel.

Analytics and Reporting

Analytics and reporting tools provide businesses with data and insights to improve their marketing automation strategy. By tracking metrics such as open and click-through rates, lead conversion rates, and customer behavior, businesses can make data-driven decisions that drive growth.

Marketing automation has rapidly transformed the way businesses market their products and services. By automating repetitive tasks, collecting and analyzing customer data, and streamlining communication channels, marketing automation has enabled businesses to better understand their customers and provide personalized experiences.

But what does the future hold for marketing automation? Here are some trends and predictions for the future of marketing automation:

Artificial Intelligence (AI) will play a larger role

Artificial intelligence (AI) is already being used in marketing automation, and this trend is set to continue. AI will be used to optimize marketing campaigns, provide personalized recommendations, and analyze large amounts of customer data to improve targeting and segmentation.

Predictive analytics will become more prevalent

Predictive analytics is the use of data, statistical algorithms, and machine learning techniques to identify the likelihood of future outcomes. In marketing automation, predictive analytics can help identify which leads are most likely to convert, which products are most likely to sell, and which channels are most effective for a particular audience.

Omni-channel marketing will be the norm

Omni-channel marketing is the use of multiple channels to reach customers, including social media, email, SMS, chatbots, and more. In the future, businesses will need to provide a seamless experience across all channels to meet customer expectations.

Account-based marketing (ABM) will continue to grow

Account-based marketing (ABM) is a targeted marketing approach that focuses on specific accounts or customers. This approach requires a deep understanding of the customer's needs and preferences, which is made possible by marketing automation tools.

Personalization will be key

Personalization is the process of tailoring marketing messages and experiences to individual customers based on their preferences and behaviors. Marketing automation enables businesses to collect and analyze customer data to provide personalized experiences at scale.

Video will become more important

Video has become a popular format for marketing content, and this trend is set to continue. Video can be used to provide engaging and informative content, and marketing automation can be used to personalize and automate the delivery of video content.

Privacy concerns will need to be addressed

As businesses collect more customer data, privacy concerns will become more important. Marketing automation tools will need to comply with data privacy regulations and provide transparency to customers about how their data is being used.

Benefits of marketing automation for modern businesses

Marketing automation is a powerful tool that can help modern businesses improve their marketing strategies, increase efficiency, and drive growth.

Here are some benefits of marketing automation for modern businesses:

Improved efficiency

Marketing automation allows businesses to automate repetitive tasks and streamline communication with customers. This can help businesses save time and resources while delivering a more consistent and effective message to customers.

Personalized experiences

Marketing automation allows businesses to collect and analyze customer data to create personalized experiences. By delivering personalized messages based on customer behavior and preferences, businesses can increase engagement and build stronger relationships with customers.

SIncreased productivity

Marketing automation tools can help businesses improve productivity by automating tasks such as lead scoring, email marketing, and social media management. This can help businesses focus on high-value tasks such as developing new products or services and building relationships with customers.

Improved lead generation and conversion

Marketing automation tools can help businesses generate and convert leads more effectively. By tracking customer behavior and delivering targeted messages, businesses can move leads through the sales funnel more efficiently and increase conversion rates.

Better customer insights

Marketing automation tools can provide businesses with valuable insights into customer behavior and preferences. By analyzing data such as website visits, email opens, and social media engagement, businesses can gain a deeper understanding of their customers and improve their marketing strategies accordingly.

Improved ROI

Marketing automation can help businesses improve their return on investment (ROI) by increasing efficiency, improving lead generation and conversion rates, and delivering personalized experiences to customers. By optimizing marketing strategies and reducing waste, businesses can achieve better results with less investment.

Examples of marketing automation in action

Marketing automation can be used in a variety of ways to improve marketing strategies and drive growth. Here are some examples of marketing automation in action:

Welcome series emails

A welcome series is a set of automated emails that are sent to new subscribers to introduce them to a business and build a relationship. The emails can include personalized messages, product recommendations, and calls-to-action that encourage engagement and lead to conversions.

Abandoned cart emails

Abandoned cart emails are automated emails that are sent to customers who have added products to their cart but haven't completed the purchase. The emails can include personalized messages, product recommendations, and incentives such as discounts or free shipping to encourage customers to complete the purchase.

Lead nurturing campaigns

Lead nurturing campaigns are a series of automated messages that are sent to leads to move them through the sales funnel. The messages can include educational content, product information, and personalized messages that help build a relationship and encourage engagement.

Social media scheduling

Social media scheduling tools allow businesses to automate the process of posting content on social media platforms. By scheduling posts in advance, businesses can ensure that they maintain a consistent presence on social media and reach a larger audience.

Dynamic content

Dynamic content allows businesses to personalize content based on customer behavior and preferences. For example, a website can display different contSent to returning visitors than to first-time visitors, or display different products to customers based on their past purchases.

Lead scoring

Lead scoring is a process of assigning values to leads based on their level of engagement and readiness to purchase. By tracking customer behavior such as website visits, email opens, and social media engagement, businesses can prioritize leads and deliver targeted messages that move them through the sales funnel.

CHAPTER 12

The Importance of Customer Experience in Marketing

In today's business world, customer experience is the key to success in marketing. It is the impression that customers have about a brand or a product, which is formed through their interactions with the brand. Customer experience (CX) is an essential part of the marketing strategy of any business because it has a significant impact on customer satisfaction, loyalty, and revenue. In this book we will discuss the importance of customer experience in marketing and how businesses can improve their CX.

Customer Experience Enhances Customer Loyalty

Customer loyalty is one of the most important factors for the success of any business. Customers who have a positive experience with a brand are more likely to remain loyal to that brand, and they are more likely to recommend it to others. By providing a great customer experience, businesses can increase customer loyalty, which can lead to increased sales and revenue.

Customer Experience Builds Brand Reputation

The customer experience is a critical factor in building a brand's reputation. Customers who have a positive experience with a brand are more likely to leave positive reviews, which can increase the brand's reputation and attract new customers. On the other hand, negative experiences can damage a brand's reputation and result in loss of business.

213

Customer Experience Increases Customer Lifetime Value

Customer lifetime value (CLV) is the amount of revenue that a customer will generate for a business over their lifetime. By providing a great customer experience, businesses can increase customer lifetime value by retaining customers and encouraging repeat business. Customers who have a positive experience are more likely to purchase from a brand again and again, which can lead to increased revenue over time.

Customer Experience Drives Word-of-Mouth Marketing

Word-of-mouth marketing is one of the most effective forms of marketing, and it is driven by the customer experience. Customers who have a positive experience with a brand are more likely to recommend it to others, which can lead to increased sales and revenue. By providing a great customer experience, businesses can encourage word-of-mouth marketing and attract new customers.

Customer Experience Increases Customer Satisfaction

Customer satisfaction is a crucial factor in the success of any business. By providing a great customer experience, businesses can increase customer satisfaction, which can lead to increased sales and revenue. Customers who are satisfied with a brand are more likely to remain loyal to that brand and recommend it to others.

Customer Experience Helps Differentiate Brands

In today's competitive business world, it is essential to differentiate a brand from its competitors. Customer experience is an excellent way to do this. By providing a unique and positive customer experience, businesses can differentiate themselves from their competitors and attract new customers.

Customer Experience Provides Valuable Customer Insights

By listening to customer feedback and monitoring customer interactions with a brand, businesses can gain valuable insights into their customers' preferences, needs, and behaviors. This information can be used to improve the customer experience and develop new products and services that better meet the needs of customers.

Customer Experience Increases Revenue

Ultimately, the customer experience can have a significant impact on revenue. By providing a great customer experience, businesses can increase customer satisfaction, loyalty, and lifetime value, which can lead to increased sales and revenue. In contrast, negative customer experiences can lead to lost sales and revenue.

Improving Customer Experience

Now that we have discussed the importance of customer experience in marketing, let's look at how businesses can improve their CX.

Develop a Customer-Centric Culture

To provide a great customer experience, businesses need to develop a customer-centric culture. This means putting the needs and preferences of customers at the center of everything the business does. All employees should be trained in customer service and have a clear understanding of the importance of the customer experience.

Personalize the Customer Experience

Personalization is key to providing a great customer experience. By tailoring

The customer experience to the individual needs and preferences of each customer, businesses can create a more engaging and memorable experience. This can be achieved through personalized communication, product recommendations, and tailored promotions.

Offer a Seamless Multichannel Experience

Customers today expect to interact with businesses through multiple channels, including social media, email, phone, and in-store. To provide a great customer experience, businesses need to offer a seamless multichannel experience that is consistent across all touchpoints.

Listen to Customer Feedback

Listening to customer feedback is crucial to improving the customer experience. Businesses should collect feedback from customers through surveys, social media, and other channels, and use this information to make improvements to the customer experience.

Invest in Technology

Technology can play a significant role in improving the customer experience. Businesses should invest in technology that can help them personalize the customer experience, offer a seamless multichannel experience, and collect and analyze customer feedback.

Train and Empower Employees

Employees are essential to delivering a great customer experience. Businesses should train and empower their employees to provide excellent customer service and make decisions that are in the best interests of the customer.

Customer experience is critical to the success of any marketing strategy. By providing a great customer experience, businesses can increase customer loyalty, build their brand reputation, increase customer lifetime value, drive word-of-mouth marketing, differentiate themselves from their competitors, gain valuable customer insights, and increase revenue. To improve the customer experience, businesses need to develop a customer-centric culture, personalize the customer experience, offer a seamless multichannel experience, listen to customer feedback, invest in technology, and train and empower employees. By doing so, businesses can create a competitive advantage and achieve long-term success.

Strategies for creating a positive customer experience

Creating a positive customer experience is essential for any business that wants to succeed in today's competitive market. It is the key to attracting new customers, retaining existing ones, and building a strong brand reputation. In this article, we will discuss some strategies for creating a positive customer experience that can help businesses improve customer satisfaction, loyalty, and ultimately, revenue.

Develop a Customer-Centric Culture

The first step in creating a positive customer experience is to develop a customer-centric culture. This means putting the customer at the center of everything the business does. All employees, from the CEO to the front-line staff, should be trained to prioritize the needs and preferences of customers. To develop a customer-centric culture, businesses should create a set of values and behaviors that reflect the importance of the customer experience. This can be achieved through training programs, company-wide communications, and recognition and rewards programs.

Personalize the Customer Experience

Personalization is key to creating a positive customer experience. Customers today expect businesses to understand their individual needs and preferences and to tailor the experience accordingly. This can be achieved through personalized communication, product recommendations, and tailored promotions.

To personalize the customer experience, businesses should collect data on customers' preferences and behaviors, such as their purchase history, browsing history, and demographic information. This data can be used to create personalized marketing campaigns and offers that are more likely to resonate with individual customers.

Offer a Seamless Multichannel Experience

Customers today expect to interact with businesses through multiple channels, including social media, email, phone, and in-store. To create a positive customer experience, businesses need to offer a seamless multichannel experience that is consistent across all touch points.

This means ensuring that customers can access the same information, products, and services regardless of the channel they are using. Businesses should also ensure that their customer service is accessible through all channels and that the service is of a consistently high standard.

Listen to Customer Feedback

Listening to customer feedback is essential to creating a positive customer experience. Customers are the best source of information about what works and what doesn't work in the customer experience. By collecting feedback from customers, businesses can identify areas for improvement and make changes that will enhance the customer experience.

To collect customer feedback, businesses can use surveys, focus groups, and social media. They should also encourage customers to provide feedback through reviews and ratings, and respond promptly to any negative feedback to address any issues and demonstrate their commitment to improving the customer experience.

Invest in Technology

Technology can play a significant role in creating a positive customer experience. It can help businesses personalize the customer experience, offer a seamless multichannel experience, and collect and analyze customer feedback.

For example, businesses can use customer relationship management (CRM) software to collect and analyze customer data, and to automate personalized marketing campaigns and customer service interactions. They can also use chatbots and virtual assistants to offer 24/7 customer service support and to handle routine queries and requests.

Train and Empower Employees

Employees are essential to creating a positive customer experience. They are the front-line staff who interact with customers every day, and they have a significant impact on the customer experience. Therefore, it is crucial to train and empower employees to provide excellent customer service and make decisions that are in the best interests of the customer.

To train employees, businesses can provide ongoing training programs that focus on customer service skills, communication skills, and problem-solving skills. They should also empower employees to make decisions that are in the best interests of the customer, such as offering refunds or replacements, and to provide feedback on the customer experience to management.

Tips for measuring and improving customer satisfaction

Measuring and improving customer satisfaction is critical for businesses to retain customers, attract new ones, and build a strong brand reputation. In this article, we will discuss some tips for measuring and improving customer satisfaction that can help businesses improve customer loyalty, reduce churn, and increase revenue.

Define Customer Satisfaction Metrics

The first step in measuring and improving customer satisfaction is to define the metrics that will be used to measure it. There are several metrics that can be used to measure customer **satisfaction, including**:

Net Promoter Score (NPS): Measures how likely customers are to recommend the business to others.

Customer Satisfaction Score (CSAT): Measures how satisfied customers are with a specific interaction or experience.

Customer Effort Score (CES): Measures how easy it was for customers to accomplish a specific task or goal.

Once the metrics have been defined, businesses should establish benchmarks and targets for each metric and track them over time.

Collect Customer Feedback

Collecting customer feedback is essential to measuring and improving customer satisfaction. There are several ways to collect customer feedback, including:

Surveys: Surveys can be sent via email, social media, or in-app to collect feedback on specific interactions or experiences.

Reviews and Ratings: Reviews and ratings can be collected on third-party review sites or through the business's website or app.

Social Media: Social media can be used to collect feedback and monitor customer sentiment.

Businesses should analyze customer feedback regularly and use it to identify areas for improvement and make changes to the customer experience.

Use Customer Feedback to Improve the Customer Experience

Once customer feedback has been collected, it should be used to improve the customer experience. This can be achieved by:

Addressing Issues: Businesses should address any issues or complaints raised by customers promptly and effectively to demonstrate their commitment to customer satisfaction.

Making Improvements: Businesses should use customer feedback to identify areas for improvement in the customer experience and make changes that will enhance it.

Celebrating Successes: Businesses should celebrate successes and share positive customer feedback with employees to reinforce the importance of customer satisfaction.

Focus on Employee Training and Development

Employees play a critical role in delivering a positive customer experience. Therefore, it is essential to focus on their training and development to improve customer satisfaction. This can be achieved by:

Providing Ongoing Training: Businesses should provide ongoing training programs that focus on customer service skills, communication skills, and problem-solving skills.

Empowering Employees: Businesses should empower employees to make decisions that are in the best interests of the customer and to provide feedback on the customer experience to management.

Recognizing and Rewarding Employees: Businesses should recognize and reward employees who demonstrate exceptional customer service skills and who contribute to improving the customer experience.

Use Technology to Improve the Customer Experience

Technology can play a significant role in improving the customer experience and measuring customer satisfaction. Businesses can use technology to:

Automate Processes: Businesses can automate customer service interactions, such as chatbots and virtual assistants, to offer 24/7 support and handle routine queries and requests.

Personalize the Customer Experience: Businesses can use customer relationship management (CRM) software to collect and analyze customer data, and to automate personalized marketing campaigns and customer service interactions.

Monitor and Analyze Customer Feedback: Businesses can use sentiment analysis tools to monitor and analyze customer feedback on social media and other channels to identify areas for improvement in the customer experience.

Offer Incentives for Customer Loyalty

Finally, businesses can offer incentives for customer loyalty to improve customer satisfaction. This can be achieved by:

Rewarding Repeat Business: Businesses can offer discounts, loyalty points, or other incentives for repeat business to encourage customer loyalty.

Offering Referral Programs: Businesses can offer referral programs to encourage existing customers to refer new customers, which can increase

CHAPTER 13

Personalizing Your Marketing Efforts

Personalizing marketing efforts is becoming increasingly important in today's competitive business landscape. Personalization allows businesses to tailor their marketing messages to individual customers based on their behavior, preferences, and interests. This can help increase engagement, improve customer loyalty, and ultimately drive sales. In this article, we will discuss some tips for personalizing your marketing efforts.

Collect Customer Data

The first step in personalizing your marketing efforts is to collect customer data. This can be achieved by:

Offering a Sign-Up Form: Include a sign-up form on your website or app that allows customers to provide information about their preferences, interests, and behavior.

Analyzing Customer Behavior: Use analytics tools to track customer behavior, such as what products they view or purchase, how they navigate your website, and how long they spend on each page.

Conducting Surveys: Send surveys to customers to gather feedback on their experience with your business and their preferences.

Segment Your Audience

Once you have collected customer data, the next step is to segment your audience based on their behavior, preferences, and interests. This can be achieved by:

Creating Customer Personas: Use the customer data you have collected to create customer personas that represent the different segments of your audience.

Analyzing Customer Behavior: Use analytics tools to identify patterns in customer behavior and segment your audience accordingly.

Tailoring Marketing Messages: Tailor your marketing messages to each segment of your audience based on their behavior, preferences, and interests.

Use Personalized Content

Personalized content can help improve customer engagement and drive sales. This can be achieved by:

Creating Personalized Product Recommendations: Use customer data and behavior to create personalized product recommendations.

Sending Personalized Emails: Send personalized emails that address customers by name, include content tailored to their interests, and offer promotions or deals based on their behavior.

Customizing Landing Pages: Create landing pages that are tailored to each segment of your audience based on their behavior, preferences, and interests.

Utilize Personalized Ads

Personalized ads can help increase engagement and drive sales. This can be achieved by:

Targeting Specific Segments: Use customer data to target specific segments of your audience with personalized ads.

Creating Custom Ads: Create custom ads that are tailored to each segment of your audience based on their behavior, preferences, and interests.

Using Dynamic Ads: Use dynamic ads that change based on the customer's behavior or preferences.

Offer Personalized Customer Service

Personalized customer service can help improve customer satisfaction and loyalty. This can be achieved by:

Offering Personalized Support: Use customer data to personalize support interactions and provide tailored solutions to customer issues.

Providing Self-Service Options: Provide self-service options, such as a knowledge base or FAQ section, that are tailored to each segment of your audience.

Using Chatbots: Use chatbots to provide 24/7 support that is tailored to each segment of your audience.

Benefits of personalized marketing

Personalized marketing, also known as one-to-one marketing, is a marketing approach that uses customer data and behavior to tailor marketing messages, products, and services to individual customers. Personalization has become increasingly important in today's competitive business landscape, as it can improve customer engagement, loyalty, and ultimately drive sales. In this article, we will discuss the benefits of personalized marketing.

Improved Customer Engagement

Personalized marketing can improve customer engagement by providing customers with content that is tailored to their interests, preferences, and behavior. By delivering personalized content, businesses can increase the likelihood of customers engaging with their brand, resulting in higher conversion rates, increased sales, and improved customer satisfaction.

For example, a retail store may use data on a customer's previous purchases to recommend similar products, or a travel company may use data on a customer's past travel history to recommend relevant vacation packages. By tailoring marketing messages to each customer, businesses can improve engagement and build stronger relationships with their customers.

Increased Customer Loyalty

Personalized marketing can also increase customer loyalty by creating a more personalized experience for customers. Customers who feel understood and appreciated are more likely to return to a business and recommend it to others.

By using customer data to tailor marketing messages and offerings to each customer, businesses can create a more personalized experience that resonates with customers. This can result in increased customer loyalty, repeat business, and improved customer lifetime value.

Higher Conversion Rates

Personalized marketing can lead to higher conversion rates by delivering tailored messages that are more relevant and appealing to customers. By using customer data to personalize marketing messages, businesses can create more effective campaigns that are more likely to convert.

For example, an email campaign that uses customer data to recommend products based on a customer's previous purchases may have a higher conversion rate than a generic email campaign. By tailoring marketing messages to each customer, businesses can increase the likelihood of conversion and drive sales.

Improved Customer Satisfaction

Personalized marketing can also improve customer satisfaction by providing customers with a more personalized experience. Customers who feel understood and appreciated are more likely to be satisfied with their experience with a business.

By tailoring marketing messages, products, and services to each customer, businesses can create a more personalized experience that resonates with customers. This can result in improved customer satisfaction, positive word-of-mouth, and improved brand reputation.

More Efficient Marketing Spend

Personalized marketing can also result in more efficient marketing spend by targeting specific segments of customers with relevant and personalized messages. By using customer data to segment the audience and deliver tailored messages, businesses can improve the effectiveness of their marketing campaigns and reduce wasted spend on irrelevant marketing messages.

For example, a marketing campaign that targets customers who have previously shown interest in a specific product may have a higher conversion rate than a generic marketing campaign that targets a broader audience. By targeting specific segments of customers with relevant and personalized messages, businesses can improve the efficiency of their marketing spend and drive better results.

Different ways to personalize marketing campaigns

Personalizing marketing campaigns can help businesses build stronger relationships with customers, improve engagement and drive sales. we will discuss different ways to personalize marketing campaigns.

Personalized Emails

Email marketing is one of the most effective ways to personalize marketing campaigns. By using customer data to segment the audience and deliver tailored messages, businesses can create more relevant and appealing email campaigns that are more likely to convert.

For example, a retailer may use data on a customer's previous purchases to recommend similar products or a travel company may use data on a customer's past travel history to recommend relevant vacation packages. By personalizing email campaigns, businesses can improve engagement and drive sales.

Dynamic Website Content

Dynamic website content is another effective way to personalize marketing campaigns. By using customer data to deliver tailored content, businesses can create a more personalized experience for each customer, increasing engagement and improving conversion rates.

For example, a retail store may use data on a customer's location to display relevant products or a travel company may use data on a customer's past travel history to display relevant vacation packages. By tailoring website content to each customer, businesses can create a more personalized experience that resonates with customers and drives sales.

Social Media Personalization

Social media platforms offer numerous opportunities for personalizing marketing campaigns. By using customer data to segment the audience and deliver tailored messages, businesses can create more effective social media campaigns that are more likely to engage customers.

For example, a retail store may use data on a customer's age, gender, and interests to deliver relevant content on social media platforms or a travel company may use data on a customer's past travel history to target them with relevant ads on social media platforms. By tailoring social media content to each customer, businesses can create a more personalized experience that resonates with customers and drives engagement.

Personalized Product Recommendations

Personalized product recommendations are another effective way to personalize marketing campaigns. By using customer data to recommend products based on their past purchases or browsing history, businesses can create more relevant and appealing product recommendations that are more likely to convert.

For example, a retailer may use data on a customer's previous purchases to recommend similar products or a travel company may use data on a customer's past travel history to recommend relevant vacation packages. By using personalized product recommendations, businesses can improve engagement and drive sales.

Personalized Ads

Personalized ads are another effective way to personalize marketing campaigns. By using customer data to deliver targeted ads, businesses can create more relevant and appealing ads that are more likely to convert.

For example, a retailer may use data on a customer's past purchases to target them with relevant ads on social media platforms or a travel company may use data on a customer's past travel history to target them with relevant ads on search engines. By using personalized ads, businesses can improve engagement and drive sales.

Personalized Offers and Promotions

Personalized offers and promotions are another effective way to personalize marketing campaigns. By using customer data to create tailored offers and promotions, businesses can create more appealing and relevant campaigns that are more likely to convert.

For example, a retailer may use data on a customer's past purchases to offer them personalized discounts or a travel company may use data on a customer's past travel history to offer them personalized vacation packages. By using personalized offers and promotions, businesses can improve engagement and drive sales.

Examples of successful personalized marketing campaigns

Successful personalized marketing campaigns have the power to create a memorable experience for customers, build loyalty, and drive sales. Here are some examples of companies that have implemented personalized marketing campaigns with great success:

Spotify's "Wrapped" Campaign

Spotify's "Wrapped" campaign is an annual personalized marketing campaign that delivers a summary of a user's listening history for the year. The campaign provides users with a detailed look at their listening habits over the year, including the top songs, artists, and genres they listened to.

The campaign is highly personalized, taking into account each user's individual listening history and creating a unique and memorable experience. The "Wrapped" campaign has been a massive success for Spotify, generating a significant amount of user engagement and driving subscriptions.

Coca-Cola's "Share a Coke" Campaign

Coca-Cola's "Share a Coke" campaign is another successful example of personalized marketing. The campaign involved replacing the Coca-Cola logo on bottles with individual names and encouraging customers to "share a Coke" with friends and family.

The campaign was highly personalized, creating a unique and memorable experience for customers who were able to find bottles with their own names or the names of friends and family members. The "Share a Coke" campaign was a massive success, increasing Coca-Cola's sales and generating a significant amount of social media engagement.

Asmazon's Personalized Recommendation

Amazon's personalized recommendation system is a prime example of how data-driven personalization can drive sales and customer engagement. The company uses data on each customer's purchase history, browsing history, and other behavioral data to deliver personalized recommendations for products that the customer is likely to be interested in.

The recommendations are highly personalized, taking into account each customer's individual preferences and creating a unique and memorable experience. Amazon's personalized recommendations have been a massive success, driving a significant amount of sales and increasing customer loyalty.

Nike's Personalized Training Programs

Nike's personalized training programs are another example of how personalization can create a memorable experience for customers. The company uses data on each customer's fitness goals, activity level, and other data points to create personalized training programs that are tailored to the individual's needs.

The personalized training programs are highly personalized, creating a unique and memorable experience for customers who are able to achieve their fitness goals with the help of Nike's personalized training programs. The personalized training programs have been a massive success for Nike, driving sales and increasing customer loyalty.

CHAPTER 14

Creating Effective Call-to-Actions

A call-to-action (CTA) is a prompt or instruction given to a user with the goal of encouraging them to take a specific action, such as making a purchase, subscribing to a newsletter, or filling out a form. CTAs are used in marketing and advertising to guide a user towards a desired conversion or goal.

The purpose of a CTA is to provide a clear and direct message to the user about what action they should take next. By using a CTA, businesses can influence the behavior of their audience and encourage them to take action towards the end goal.

CTAs can be used in a variety of marketing channels, including email marketing, social media, website content, and advertisements. They are typically designed to stand out from the surrounding content and grab the user's attention.

CTAs can take many forms, including buttons, links, images, or text. The most effective CTAs are clear and concise, using action-oriented language that encourages the user to take the desired action. Examples of effective CTA language include "Sign up now," "Get your free trial," or "Buy now."

Effective CTAs should also be relevant to the user and aligned with their interests and needs. For example, a CTA for a fitness app might use language such as "Get in shape for summer" or "Achieve your fitness goals" to appeal to users who are interested in fitness.

Another important aspect of CTAs is their placement on a page or within an email. They should be prominently displayed and easily accessible to the user. In email marketing, for example, CTAs are typically placed near the top of the email to ensure they are seen by the user before they lose interest or stop reading.

Best practices for creating effective CTAs

Creating effective call-to-actions (CTAs) is crucial for driving conversions and achieving marketing goals. Here are some best practices for creating effective CTAs:

Use Action-Oriented Language

The language used in a CTA should be action-oriented, using verbs that encourage users to take action. Using words like "buy," "subscribe," or "download" can help make it clear what action the user should take next.

Be Clear and Concise

The CTA should be clear and concise, providing a simple and direct message to the user. Avoid using vague or ambiguous language that might confuse or frustrate the user.

Create Urgency

Adding urgency to a CTA can encourage users to take action quickly. Using phrases like "limited time offer" or "while supplies last" can create a sense of urgency and motivate users to act quickly.

Make it stand out

The CTA should be prominently displayed and stand out from the surrounding content. Using contrasting colors, bold text, or a larger font size can help draw the user's attention to the CTA.

Be Relevant

The CTA should be relevant to the user and aligned with their interests and needs. Personalizing the CTA based on the user's browsing or purchase history can make it more relevant and increase the likelihood of a conversion.

Test and Refine

Testing different versions of the CTA can help determine which one is most effective at driving conversions. Testing elements like language, placement, and design can help refine the CTA and improve its effectiveness.

Use a Strong Design

The design of the CTA can have a significant impact on its effectiveness. Using a strong design that is visually appealing and aligned with the brand's aesthetic can help increase conversions.

Consider Placement

The placement of the CTA can also have a significant impact on its effectiveness. Placing the CTA in a prominent location, such as above the fold or at the end of a blog post, can help increase its visibility and drive conversions.

Align with the Landing Page

The CTA should be aligned with the landing page and provide a clear and direct continuation of the user's journey. Using language and design that is consistent with the landing page can help create a seamless user experience and increase conversions.

Monitor and Analyze Performance

Tracking the performance of the CTA can help determine its effectiveness and identify areas for improvement. Monitoring metrics like click-through rates and conversion rates can provide valuable insights and help refine the CTA over time.

Examples of successful CTAs

Here are some examples of successful call-to-action (CTA) buttons used by various businesses:

Airbnb

Airbnb uses a simple yet effective CTA on its homepage that reads "Become a Host." The CTA button is prominently displayed and uses a contrasting color to stand out from the rest of the content. The language used in the CTA is action-oriented and clear, encouraging users to take the next step to become a host.

HubSpot

HubSpot uses a personalized CTA on its website that changes depending on the user's browsing history. For example, if a user has been browsing content related to email marketing, the CTA might read "Get Email Marketing Tips." This personalized approach makes the CTA more relevant to the user and increases the likelihood of a conversion.

Squarespace

Squarespace uses a CTA on its homepage that reads "Get Started." The CTA is prominently displayed and uses a contrasting color to draw the user's attention. The language used in the CTA is clear and concise, making it easy for users to understand what action they should take next.

Dropbox

Dropbox uses a CTA on its homepage that reads "Sign Up for Free." The CTA is prominently displayed and uses a contrasting color to stand out from the rest of the content. The language used in the CTA is action-oriented and clear, encouraging users to take the next step to sign up for the service.

Spotify

Spotify uses a CTA on its website that encourages users to sign up for a free trial of its premium service. The CTA reads "Get Premium Free for 1 Month" and is prominently displayed on the homepage. The language used in the CTA creates a sense of urgency, encouraging users to take advantage of the free trial offer.

Grammarly

Grammarly uses a CTA on its website that encourages users to download its browser extension. The CTA reads "Add to Chrome It's free" and is prominently displayed on the homepage. The language used in the CTA is action-oriented and clear, making it easy for users to understand what action they should take next.

Trello

Trello uses a CTA on its homepage that encourages users to sign up for its service. The CTA reads "Sign Up - It's Free" and is prominently displayed on the homepage. The language used in the CTA is clear and concise, making it easy for users to understand what action they should take next.

Slack

Slack uses a CTA on its homepage that encourages users to sign up for its service. The CTA reads "Get Started for Free" and is prominently displayed on the homepage. The language used in the CTA is action-oriented and clear, encouraging users to take the next step to sign up for the service.

Asana

Asana uses a CTA on its homepage that encourages users to sign up for its service. The CTA reads "Try Asana for Free" and is prominently displayed on the homepage. The language used in the CTA is clear and concise, making it easy for users to understand what action they should take next.

Mailchimp

Mailchimp uses a CTA on its homepage that encourages users to sign up for its service. The CTA reads "Sign Up Free" and is prominently displayed on the homepage. The language used in the CTA is action-oriented and clear, encouraging users to take the next step to sign up for the service.

CHAPTER 15

Developing a Marketing Plan

Marketing planning is the process of creating a roadmap that outlines the steps a business will take to achieve its marketing goals. It is a crucial element of any successful marketing strategy, as it helps businesses to allocate resources and stay focused on achieving their objectives. The marketing planning process typically involves several stages, including:

Situation Analysis

The first stage of the marketing planning process involves analyzing the current situation to identify strengths, weaknesses, opportunities, and threats (SWOT). This involves gathering data about the market, competitors, target audience, and the company's current marketing efforts. This analysis helps businesses to gain an understanding of their position in the market and identify areas for improvement.

Market Segmentation and Targeting

The next stage involves identifying and dividing the market into different segments based on shared characteristics such as demographics, interests, and behaviors. The goal is to identify the segments that are most likely to be interested in the company's products or services and to target them with tailored marketing messages.

Setting Marketing Objectives

The third stage involves setting specific, measurable, achievable, relevant, and time-bound (SMART) marketing objectives. These objectives should be aligned with the company's overall business goals and should be designed to achieve a specific outcome, such as increasing sales, building brand awareness, or driving website traffic.

Developing Marketing Strategies

The next stage involves developing marketing strategies that are designed to achieve the objectives set out in the previous stage. These strategies may include tactics such as social media marketing, content marketing, email marketing, paid advertising, and search engine optimization (SEO). The goal is to identify the most effective marketing channels for reaching the target audience and to create a plan for how to execute these strategies.

Implementing Marketing Tactics

The fifth stage involves implementing the marketing tactics identified in the previous stage. This may involve creating content, designing advertising campaigns, developing social media posts, and running email marketing campaigns. It is important to track the performance of these tactics and make adjustments as necessary to ensure they are effective in achieving the objectives set out in the earlier stages.

Measuring and Evaluating Results

The final stage involves measuring and evaluating the results of the marketing efforts. This involves tracking key performance indicators (KPIs) such as website traffic, social media engagement, and sales. It is important to use this data to evaluate the effectiveness of the marketing tactics and make adjustments as necessary to improve future campaigns.

Key components of a marketing plan

A marketing plan is a comprehensive document that outlines a business's marketing strategies, objectives, and tactics. It serves as a roadmap that guides a company's marketing efforts and helps them to achieve their goals. The key components of a marketing plan include:

Executive Summary

The executive summary is a brief overview of the marketing plan, outlining the key objectives, strategies, and tactics. It should be concise, clear, and compelling, and should provide a snapshot of the marketing plan for stakeholders.

Situation Analysis

The situation analysis involves researching the market, competitors, and target audience to understand the current business environment. This section should include an analysis of the company's strengths, weaknesses, opportunities, and threats (SWOT analysis) to help identify the key areas of focus.

Target Audience

The target audience is the group of consumers that the company aims to reach with their marketing efforts. This section should include a detailed description of the target audience's demographics, psychographics, and behaviors, as well as their pain points and motivations.

Marketing Objectives

Marketing objectives should be specific, measurable, achievable, relevant, and time-bound (SMART). This section should outline the objectives that the marketing plan aims to achieve, such as increasing brand awareness, driving website traffic, or increasing sales.

Marketing Strategies

Marketing strategies are the broad approaches that the business will use to achieve its marketing objectives. This section should include a detailed explanation of the key strategies, such as content marketing, social media marketing, or paid advertising.

Marketing Tactics

Marketing tactics are the specific activities that the business will undertake to implement the marketing strategies. This section should include a detailed explanation of the marketing tactics, such as creating blog posts, designing social media posts, or running email marketing campaigns.

Budget and Resources

The budget and resources section should outline the resources required to execute the marketing plan, including the budget, staff, and tools needed. This section should also include a detailed explanation of how the budget will be allocated across the different marketing tactics.

Timeline and Milestones

The timeline and milestones section should outline the timeline for implementing the marketing plan, including key milestones and deadlines. This section should also include details of how progress will be tracked and reported on.

Metrics and Evaluation

The metrics and evaluation section should outline the key performance indicators (KPIs) that will be used to track the success of the marketing plan. This section should also include a plan for how the KPIs will be measured and evaluated.

Tips for developing a successful marketing plan

Developing a successful marketing plan can be a complex process, but with the right approach, it can help businesses achieve their marketing objectives and drive success. Here are some tips for developing a successful marketing plan:

Define Your Marketing Objectives

Before creating your marketing plan, it's important to define your marketing objectives. This means identifying what you want to achieve through your marketing efforts, such as increasing brand awareness, driving website traffic, or generating sales. Your marketing objectives should be specific, measurable, achievable, relevant, and time-bound (SMART).

Conduct a Situational Analysis

Conducting a situational analysis involves researching your market, competitors, and target audience to understand the current business environment. This analysis should include an assessment of your company's strengths, weaknesses, opportunities, and threats (SWOT analysis). Understanding the competitive landscape and your target audience's needs and preferences can help you identify key areas of focus for your marketing plan.

Know Your Target Audience

To create a successful marketing plan, you need to know your target audience intimately. This means understanding their demographics, psychographics, behaviors, and preferences.

This information can help you tailor your messaging, positioning, and marketing tactics to resonate with your target audience and drive engagement.

Develop Your Marketing Strategies

Based on your marketing objectives, situational analysis, and target audience insights, you can start developing your marketing strategies. Your strategies should be broad approaches that will help you achieve your marketing objectives, such as content marketing, social media marketing, or paid advertising.

Create Your Marketing Tactics

Once you have defined your marketing strategies, you can start creating your marketing tactics. These are the specific activities that you will undertake to implement your marketing strategies, such as creating blog posts, designing social media posts, or running email marketing campaigns. Your marketing tactics should be tailored to your target audience and aligned with your marketing objectives and strategies.

Allocate Your Budget and Resources

Creating a successful marketing plan requires the right resources, including budget, staff, and tools. Allocating your budget and resources effectively is crucial to ensure that you can execute your marketing tactics and achieve your marketing objectives. You should also consider the ROI of each marketing tactic to ensure that you are investing your budget wisely.

Develop Your Timeline and Milestones

Creating a timeline and milestones for your marketing plan can help you stay on track and ensure that your marketing tactics are executed in a timely manner. This timeline should include key milestones and deadlines, as well as details of how progress will be tracked and reported on.

Monitor and Evaluate Your Results

To ensure that your marketing plan is driving success, it's important to monitor and evaluate your results regularly. This involves tracking your key performance indicators (KPIs), such as website traffic, conversion rates, and customer acquisition costs, and using this data to make informed decisions about your marketing strategies and tactics.

CHAPTER 16

Measuring Marketing Effectiveness

Measuring marketing effectiveness is critical for businesses to evaluate the success of their marketing campaigns and make informed decisions on how to optimize their strategies for better results. Here are some different metrics that businesses can use to measure the effectiveness of their marketing efforts:

Return on Investment (ROI)

ROI measures the financial return generated from a marketing campaign. It compares the cost of the campaign to the revenue generated from the campaign. A positive ROI indicates that the campaign has generated more revenue than it cost, while a negative ROI indicates that the campaign lost money.

Conversion Rate

Conversion rate measures the percentage of website visitors who take a desired action, such as making a purchase or filling out a form. A higher conversion rate indicates that the marketing campaign is effective in converting website visitors into customers or leads.

Cost per Acquisition (CPA)

CPA measures the cost of acquiring a new customer or lead. It takes into account the cost of the marketing campaign and the number of new customers or leads generated. A lower CPA indicates that the marketing campaign is more cost-effective in acquiring new customers or leads.

Customer Lifetime Value (CLV)

CLV measures the total revenue generated from a customer over their lifetime with a business. A higher CLV indicates that the marketing campaign is effective in generating loyal customers who generate more revenue over time.

Website Traffic

Website traffic measures the number of visitors to a website. It can indicate the effectiveness of a marketing campaign in generating awareness and interest in a business.

Social Media Engagement

Social media engagement measures the level of interaction on a business's social media accounts, such as likes, comments, and shares. It can indicate the effectiveness of a social media marketing campaign in engaging with target audiences.

Brand Awareness

Brand awareness measures the level of familiarity that customers have with a brand. It can be measured through surveys, social media mentions, and website traffic. A higher level of brand awareness indicates that the marketing campaign is effective in increasing the visibility of the brand.

Customer Satisfaction

Customer satisfaction measures the level of satisfaction that customers have with a business's products or services. It can be measured through surveys and customer reviews. A higher level of customer satisfaction indicates that the marketing campaign is effective in meeting customer needs and expectations.

Tools and techniques for tracking and analyzing marketing data

In today's digital age, tracking and analyzing marketing data is essential for businesses to make informed decisions and optimize their marketing strategies for better results. Here are some tools and techniques that businesses can use to track and analyze marketing data:

Google Analytics

Google Analytics is a web analytics service that tracks and reports website traffic. It provides businesses with detailed information about their website visitors, including demographics, location, and behavior. Google Analytics can also track the effectiveness of marketing campaigns, including conversion rates and ROI.

Social Media Analytics

Social media analytics tools track and analyze the performance of social media marketing campaigns. They provide businesses with insights into the engagement and reach of their social media content, including likes, shares, comments, and followers.

Email Marketing Analytics

Email marketing analytics tools track and analyze the performance of email marketing campaigns. They provide businesses with insights into the open rates, click-through rates, and conversion rates of their email campaigns.

Customer Relationship Management (CRM) Software

CRM software is used to manage and analyze customer interactions and data throughout the customer lifecycle. It can track customer behavior, preferences, and purchases, as well as provide insights into customer retention and loyalty.

Heatmaps

Heatmaps are visual representations of website visitor behavior, showing where visitors click, scroll, and spend the most time on a website. Heatmaps can provide businesses with insights into website usability, design, and content, and can help optimize website performance and conversion rates.

A/B Testing

A/B testing involves creating two versions of a marketing campaign, such as a website or email, and testing them with different audiences to see which performs better. A/B testing can provide businesses with insights into the effectiveness of different marketing strategies and help optimize campaigns for better results.

Surveys and Feedback

Surveys and feedback can provide businesses with direct insights into customer preferences, opinions, and behavior. They can be used to gather feedback on marketing campaigns, product development, and customer satisfaction.

Marketing Automation

Marketing automation tools can automate repetitive marketing tasks, such as email campaigns and social media posting, and track the performance of these campaigns. Marketing automation can save businesses time and resources, as well as provide insights into campaign effectiveness.

Best practices for using data to improve marketing strategies

Using data to improve marketing strategies is crucial in today's digital age. Here are some best practices for using data to optimize marketing strategies:

Define clear goals and KPIs

Before analyzing any data, businesses should define clear goals and key performance indicators (KPIs) to measure success. Goals should be specific, measurable, achievable, relevant, and time-bound (SMART). KPIs should be aligned with these goals and should be measurable and meaningful to the business.

Collect and consolidate relevant data

Businesses should collect and consolidate relevant data from various sources, including website analytics, social media analytics, email marketing analytics, CRM software, and customer feedback. This data should be organized and analyzed to provide insights into customer behavior, preferences, and trends.

Use data visualization tools

Data visualization tools, such as charts, graphs, and dashboards, can help businesses make sense of complex data and identify trends and patterns. These tools can also help communicate insights to stakeholders in a clear and concise manner.

Conduct regular data analysis

Data analysis should be conducted regularly to monitor performance and identify opportunities for improvement. Businesses should track KPIs and analyze trends over time to identify areas for improvement and make data-driven decisions.

Experiment and test

Businesses should experiment and test different marketing strategies to identify what works and what doesn't. A/B testing, for example, can help identify which marketing campaigns and tactics drive the best results.

Continuously optimize and iterate

Based on data insights and experimentation, businesses should continuously optimize and iterate their marketing strategies to improve performance. This may involve adjusting messaging, targeting, channels, or tactics to better align with customer preferences and behavior.

Invest in data and analytics talent

To effectively use data to optimize marketing strategies, businesses should invest in data and analytics talent. This may involve hiring data analysts, data scientists, or marketing analysts to manage and analyze data and provide insights and recommendations to inform marketing strategies.

CHAPTER 17

Budgeting for Marketing Success

Marketing is an essential component of any business, but it can also be one of the most costly. To ensure that your marketing efforts are effective and efficient, it's important to create a comprehensive marketing budget. Here are some tips for budgeting for marketing success:

Define your marketing goals and objectives

Before creating a marketing budget, it's essential to define your marketing goals and objectives. This will help you determine which marketing tactics and channels to focus on and how much to allocate to each one.

Determine your total marketing budget

Once you have defined your marketing goals and objectives, you need to determine your total marketing budget. This will depend on various factors, including the size of your business, the industry you operate in, and the overall marketing landscape.

Allocate your budget across different marketing channels

Once you have determined your total marketing budget, you need to allocate it across different marketing channels. This may include social media advertising, email marketing, content marketing, paid search advertising, public relations, and events. The allocation will depend on your goals, target audience, and the effectiveness of each channel.

Track your spending and adjust your budget as necessary

It's essential to track your spending and adjust your budget as necessary to ensure that you're getting the most out of your marketing efforts. This may involve scaling back on channels that aren't producing results or increasing spending on those that are performing well.

Consider both short-term and long-term marketing goals

When creating a marketing budget, it's important to consider both short-term and long-term marketing goals. While short-term goals may focus on driving immediate sales, long-term goals may focus on building brand awareness and loyalty.

Invest in marketing analytics tools

Investing in marketing analytics tools can help you track the effectiveness of your marketing efforts and make data-driven decisions. These tools can provide insights into customer behavior, campaign performance, and ROI.

Consider outsourcing your marketing efforts

Outsourcing your marketing efforts can be a cost-effective way to access the expertise and resources you need to achieve your marketing goals. This may include working with an agency or freelancer to develop and execute marketing campaigns.

budgeting for marketing success requires careful planning and strategic allocation of resources. By defining your marketing goals and objectives, determining your total marketing budget, allocating your budget across different marketing channels, tracking your spending and adjusting as necessary, considering both short-term and long-term goals, investing in marketing analytics tools, and considering outsourcing your marketing efforts, you can create a comprehensive marketing budget that drives success.

Importance of budgeting for marketing

Budgeting is a crucial aspect of any business, including marketing. A well-planned and executed marketing budget can help companies achieve their marketing goals while managing their expenses effectively. Here are some reasons why budgeting for marketing is important:

Setting priorities

Budgeting helps to set priorities for marketing activities. By having a budget in place, companies can decide which marketing Sstrategies to invest in and which ones to eliminate or reduce. This helps to ensure that the company's marketing efforts are aligned with its overall business goals and objectives.

Managing expenses

A marketing budget helps to manage expenses effectively. By knowing how much money is available for marketing activities, companies can make informed decisions about how to allocate their resources. This helps to prevent overspending and ensures that the company is using its marketing budget in the most efficient way possible.

Maximizing return on investment

Budgeting for marketing helps to maximize return on investment (ROI). By setting clear goals and objectives, companies can track their progress and determine which marketing activities are delivering the best ROI. This enables them to make adjustments and reallocate their resources to the most effective marketing strategies.

Aligning marketing activities with business goals

Marketing activities should be aligned with the overall business goals and objectives. Budgeting for marketing helps to ensure that marketing activities are in line with the company's strategic plan. This helps to create a cohesive and effective marketing plan that drives the company towards its goals.

Enhancing decision-making

A marketing budget helps to enhance decision-making. By having a clear understanding of the resources available, companies can make informed decisions about which marketing activities to pursue and which ones to avoid. This helps to prevent wasted resources and ensures that the company's marketing efforts are aligned with its overall business objectives.

Identifying opportunities

Budgeting for marketing can help to identify new opportunities for growth. By analyzing the effectiveness of current marketing strategies and tracking the ROI of different activities, companies can identify new opportunities to reach their target audience and expand their customer base. This helps to drive growth and increase revenue.

Budgeting for marketing is a critical aspect of any successful business. It helps to set priorities, manage expenses effectively, maximize ROI, align marketing activities with business goals, enhance decision-making, and identify new opportunities for growth. By creating a comprehensive marketing budget, companies can ensure that their marketing efforts are aligned with their overall business objectives and achieve the best possible results from their marketing activities.

Different budgeting approaches

When it comes to budgeting for marketing, there are several different approaches that businesses can take. The right approach will depend on the specific needs and goals of the company. Here are some of the most common budgeting approaches:

Percentage of revenue

The percentage of revenue approach involves allocating a percentage of the company's total revenue towards marketing. The percentage can vary depending on the industry, the company's size, and other factors. This approach is popular because it ensures that the marketing budget scales with the size of the business.

Fixed budget

A fixed budget involves setting a specific dollar amount for the marketing budget, which does not change regardless of changes in revenue or other factors. This approach provides certainty and predictability in budgeting, which can be helpful for businesses with limited resources.

Competitive parity

The competitive parity approach involves setting the marketing budget based on what competitors are spending. The idea is to match or exceed the amount that competitors are spending on marketing in order to stay competitive. This approach is useful for businesses in highly competitive markets.

Objective and task-based

Objective and task-based budgeting involves setting a budget based on specific marketing goals and the tasks required to achieve those goals. This approach requires a detailed analysis of marketing objectives, strategies, and tactics, and can be more time-consuming than other budgeting methods. However, it provides a more customized and targeted approach to budgeting.

ROI-based

An ROI-based budgeting approach involves allocating the marketing budget based on the expected return on investment (ROI) of different marketing activities. This approach requires a thorough understanding of the potential ROI of each marketing strategy, and the ability to track and measure the effectiveness of different campaigns.

Zero-based

A zero-based budgeting approach involves starting with a zero budget and then building it up from scratch based on specific marketing goals and objectives. This approach requires a detailed analysis of all marketing activities, and can be time-consuming. However, it allows for a thorough review of all marketing expenses and can help to identify areas where expenses can be reduced or eliminated.

Percentage of revenue

The percentage of revenue approach is a popular method for small businesses that have a consistent revenue stream. This approach allows businesses to allocate a set percentage of their revenue towards marketing, which can help ensure that they are investing enough in their marketing efforts to stay competitive. The percentage allocated can vary depending on the industry, the size of the business, and other factors.

One potential disadvantage of this approach is that it does not take into account the specific needs or goals of the business. For example, a company that is just starting out may need to invest more heavily in marketing in order to build brand awareness and attract customers, whereas a more established company may be able to allocate a smaller percentage of their revenue towards marketing.

Fixed budget

A fixed budget is a good option for businesses that want to have more control over their marketing expenses. With a fixed budget, the company sets a specific dollar amount that they are willing to spend on marketing, and then sticks to that amount regardless of changes in revenue or other factors.

One of the benefits of this approach is that it provides a more predictable and stable budget. However, it can also be more difficult to adjust the budget if unexpected opportunities or challenges arise.

Competitive parity

The competitive parity approach involves setting the marketing budget based on what competitors are spending. This approach can be useful for businesses that are in highly competitive industries, as it allows them to stay competitive with other companies that are spending similar amounts on marketing.

However, this approach does not take into account the specific needs or goals of the business, and may not be appropriate for businesses that are trying to differentiate themselves from competitors.

Objective and task-based

Objective and task-based budgeting involves setting a budget based on specific marketing goals and the tasks required to achieve those goals. This approach requires a detailed analysis of marketing objectives, strategies, and tactics, and can be more time-consuming than other budgeting methods. However, it provides a more customized and targeted approach to budgeting.

By setting specific objectives and identifying the tasks required to achieve them, businesses can ensure that they are investing in marketing activities that are aligned with their overall business goals. This approach also allows for greater flexibility in adjusting the budget as needed.

ROI-based

An ROI-based budgeting approach involves allocating the marketing budget based on the expected return on investment (ROI) of different marketing activities. This approach requires a thorough understanding of the potential ROI of each marketing strategy, and the ability to track and measure the effectiveness of different campaigns.

By investing in marketing activities that are expected to generate the highest ROI, businesses can maximize their marketing budget and ensure that they are investing in activities that are most likely to drive growth. However, this approach can be more difficult to implement, as it requires a thorough understanding of the potential ROI of different marketing activities.

Zero-based

A zero-based budgeting approach involves starting with a zero budget and then building it up from scratch based on specific marketing goals and objectives. This approach requires a

299

detailed analysis of all marketing activities, and can be time-consuming. However, it allows for a thorough review of all marketing expenses and can help to identify areas where expenses can be reduced or eliminated.

By starting with a zero budget and then evaluating each marketing activity based on its potential ROI and alignment with business goals, businesses can ensure that they are investing their marketing budget in the most effective way possible.

the right budgeting approach will depend on the specific needs and goals of the business. By carefully considering the available options and selecting the approach that best fits their needs, businesses can create a successful marketing budget that maximizes ROI and drives growth.

Tips for creating a realistic marketing budget

Creating a realistic marketing budget can be a daunting task, especially if you are new to marketing or working with a limited budget. However, a well-planned and executed marketing budget is essential for the success of any marketing campaign. Here are some tips to help you create a realistic marketing budget:

Define your marketing goals: Before creating a budget, it is essential to define your marketing goals. What do you want to achieve through your marketing campaign? Do you want to increase brand awareness, generate leads, or drive sales? Once you have defined your marketing goals, you can determine the budget needed to achieve those goals.

Understand your target audience: Knowing your target audience is essential for creating an effective marketing campaign. It also helps you

301

to determine how much you should allocate towards your marketing budget. Understanding your target audience will allow you to select the most effective marketing channels to reach them.

Prioritize your marketing tactics: Not all marketing tactics are created equal. Some tactics are more expensive than others. It is essential to prioritize your marketing tactics based on their effectiveness and cost. For example, if you have a limited budget, it may be more cost-effective to invest in content marketing rather than expensive paid advertising.

Set a budget that aligns with your revenue goals: Your marketing budget should be aligned with your revenue goals. A general rule of thumb is to allocate between 5-10% of your revenue towards marketing. However, this can vary depending on your industry and the size of your business.

Consider your marketing mix: Your marketing mix includes all the channels and tactics that you use to reach your target audience. Your marketing budget should be divided among these channels based on their effectiveness and cost. For example, if social media is a significant driver of traffic and conversions for your business, you may want to allocate a larger portion of your budget towards social media marketing.

Plan for unexpected expenses: It is essential to plan for unexpected expenses when creating a marketing budget. Marketing campaigns can be unpredictable, and unexpected expenses can arise. Be sure to allocate some of your budget towards contingencies to ensure that you are prepared for any unforeseen costs.

Track and adjust your budget as needed: It is crucial to track your marketing budget regularly to ensure that you are staying on track and meeting your goals. If you find that certain tactics are not working, you may need to adjust your budget accordingly. Tracking your budget also allows you to make data-driven decisions and optimize your marketing campaign for maximum effectiveness.

CHAPTER 18

The Ethics of Marketing

Marketing is an essential aspect of any business, but it is important to consider the ethics of marketing. Ethics in marketing refers to the principles and values that guide the conduct of marketers in their interactions with customers, competitors, and other stakeholders. In recent years, the importance of ethical marketing has grown, as consumers have become more aware of corporate social responsibility and the impact of their purchasing decisions on society and the environment. Here are some key considerations for ethical marketing:

Honesty and transparency: Honesty and transparency are essential components of ethical marketing. Marketers must provide accurate and truthful information about their products and services, and avoid making false or misleading claims. This includes being transparent about the potential risks and limitations of their products, as well as disclosing any conflicts of interest.

Respect for privacy: Marketers must respect the privacy of their customers and protect their personal information. This includes obtaining consent before collecting or using personal information, and providing clear information about how the information will be used.

Fair competition: Ethical marketing requires fair competition and respect for the rights of competitors. This means avoiding unfair or deceptive practices, such as spreading false rumors about competitors, stealing trade secrets, or engaging in price fixing.

Social responsibility: Ethical marketing requires a commitment to social responsibility and the well-being of society and the environment. This means taking steps to reduce the environmental impact of products and services, supporting ethical labor practices, and contributing to community development.

Cultural sensitivity: Ethical marketing also requires cultural sensitivity and respect for diversity. Marketers must be aware of cultural norms and values, and avoid using language or imagery that is offensive or disrespectful.

Informed consent: Ethical marketing requires obtaining informed consent from customers before engaging in marketing activities. This includes providing clear and accurate information about the products and services being offered, as well as any potential risks or limitations.

Monitoring and accountability: Ethical marketing requires ongoing monitoring and accountability to ensure that ethical standards are being met. This includes establishing clear policies and procedures for ethical marketing, as well as monitoring compliance and addressing any ethical violations.

Importance of ethical marketing practices

Ethical marketing practices are essential for building trust and credibility with customers, fostering a positive brand image, and promoting the long-term success of businesses. Here are some key reasons why ethical marketing is important:

Building trust and credibility: Ethical marketing practices can help businesses build trust and credibility with customers. By providing accurate and truthful information about products and services, avoiding deceptive or manipulative marketing tactics, and demonstrating a commitment to social responsibility and ethical behavior, businesses can establish themselves as trustworthy and reliable partners for their customers.

Fostering a positive brand image: Ethical marketing practices can also help businesses build a positive brand image. Consumers today are more aware than ever of issues such as corporate social responsibility and sustainability, and are more likely to support companies that share their values. By demonstrating a commitment to ethical behavior and social responsibility, businesses can differentiate themselves from competitors and build a positive reputation in the marketplace.

Avoiding legal and financial risks: Unethical marketing practices can also expose businesses to legal and financial risks. For example, false or misleading advertising can lead to lawsuits or fines, and can damage a company's reputation. By following ethical marketing practices and complying with laws and regulations, businesses can avoid these risks and protect themselves from legal and financial liability.

Meeting consumer expectations: Consumers today have high expectations for ethical behavior from businesses. In a recent survey,

71% of consumers said they expect companies to take a stance on social and environmental issues, and 83% said they expect companies to behave ethically. By meeting these expectations and demonstrating a commitment to ethical behavior, businesses can build stronger relationships with customers and enhance their brand reputation.

Promoting long-term success: Ethical marketing practices can also contribute to the long-term success of businesses. By building trust and credibility with customers, fostering a positive brand image, avoiding legal and financial risks, and meeting consumer expectations, businesses can create a sustainable competitive advantage and drive long-term growth and profitability.

ethical marketing practices are essential for building trust and credibility with customers, fostering a positive brand image, and promoting the long-term success of businesses. By following ethical principles and demonstrating a commitment to social responsibility and ethical behavior, businesses can differentiate themselves from competitors, build a loyal customer base, and contribute to the well-being of society and the environment.

Examples of unethical marketing practices

Unethical marketing practices can take many forms and can be detrimental to both consumers and businesses. Here are some common examples of unethical marketing practices:

Deceptive advertising: Deceptive advertising is a form of false advertising that intentionally misleads consumers by making false or misleading claims about a product or service. This can include using exaggerated language or images, making unsubstantiated claims, or omitting important information about the product or service.

Bait-and-switch advertising: Bait-and-switch advertising is a deceptive marketing tactic that involves luring consumers in with a low-priced product or service and then trying to sell them a more expensive alternative. This tactic is often used in the retail industry, where consumers may be enticed by a sale or promotional offer but then find that the advertised product is out of stock or unavailable.

Price fixing: Price fixing is an illegal marketing practice that involves colluding with competitors to set prices for products or services. This can result in consumers paying higher prices for products or services than they would in a competitive market.

False endorsements: False endorsements occur when a business or individual makes false or misleading claims about the effectiveness or benefits of a product or service. This can include using fake testimonials or endorsements, or misrepresenting the credentials or qualifications of the endorser.

Privacy violations: Privacy violations occur when a business collects, uses, or shares personal information about consumers without their consent. This can include tracking consumer behavior online, sharing personal information with third parties, or using personal information for purposes other than those for which it was collected.

Exploitative marketing to vulnerable populations: Exploitative marketing involves targeting vulnerable populations, such as children or the elderly, with deceptive or manipulative marketing tactics. This can include using misleading language or imagery, or promoting products or services that are harmful or unsafe.

Cultural insensitivity: Cultural insensitivity occurs when a business uses language or imagery that is offensive or insensitive to particular cultural groups. This can include using stereotypes or caricatures that reinforce negative cultural attitudes, or using language or imagery that is disrespectful or offensive to a particular group.

Best practices for ensuring ethical marketing practices

Ethical marketing practices are essential for building trust and credibility with customers and promoting the long-term success of businesses. Here are some best practices for ensuring ethical marketing practices:

Be honest and transparent: Honesty and transparency are key principles of ethical marketing. Businesses should be upfront about the benefits and limitations of their products or services, and avoid making exaggerated or false claims.

Protect consumer privacy: Businesses should take steps to protect consumer privacy, such as obtaining consent for data collection and use, and implementing strong data security measures.

Avoid discrimination and exploitation: Businesses should avoid targeting vulnerable populations with exploitative marketing tactics, and should be sensitive to cultural differences and diversity in their marketing communications.

Follow industry regulations and guidelines: Businesses should be aware of and comply with industry regulations and guidelines, such as the Federal Trade Commission's rules on false advertising and deceptive marketing practices.

Train employees on ethical marketing practices: Businesses should provide training and education to employees on ethical marketing practices, including how to avoid deceptive or manipulative tactics and how to protect consumer privacy.

Monitor and address ethical violations: Businesses should monitor their marketing practices and take prompt action to address any ethical violations, such as false or misleading advertising.

Foster a culture of ethics and integrity: Finally, businesses should promote a culture of ethics and integrity throughout their organization, emphasizing the importance of ethical behavior and encouraging employees to speak up about any ethical concerns.

CHAPTER 19

Conclusion

Understanding the importance of customer experience in marketing, and strategies for creating a positive customer experience.

Personalizing marketing efforts to improve engagement and build customer relationships.

Creating effective calls-to-action (CTAs) that encourage customer action.

Developing a successful marketing plan, including key components and tips for success.

Measuring marketing effectiveness through various metrics and tools, and using data to improve marketing strategies.

Budgeting for marketing success, including different budgeting approaches and tips for creating a realistic marketing budget.

Ensuring ethical marketing practices, including the importance of honesty, transparency, and protecting consumer privacy, and best practices for fostering a culture of ethics and integrity.

Overall, this book emphasized the importance of understanding and meeting customer needs, building strong relationships based on trust and transparency, and continuously improving marketing strategies through data analysis and ethical practices.

Revolutionizing marketing for modern businesses requires a focus on customer-centricity, personalization, data-driven decision-making, and ethical practices. By placing the customer at the center of marketing strategies and using data to drive insights and decisions, businesses can create more targeted and effective marketing campaigns that improve customer engagement, loyalty, and satisfaction.

Personalization is also critical in modern marketing, as customers expect more personalized experiences and communications from businesses. By leveraging data and technology to personalize messaging and interactions, businesses can improve engagement and build stronger customer relationships.

Finally, ethical practices are essential for building trust and credibility with customers, and for promoting the long-term success of businesses. By following best practices for ethical marketing, businesses can establish themselves as trustworthy and transparent, and build long-term relationships with customers based on mutual respect and value.

Overall, revolutionizing marketing for modern businesses requires a commitment to continuous improvement and a willingness to adapt to changing customer needs and preferences. By embracing customer-centricity, personalization, data-driven decision-making, and ethical practices, businesses can succeed in today's rapidly changing marketing landscape and build long-term success.